SOFTWARE TESTING

Fundamental Principles and Essential Knowledge

James McCaffrey

ISBN: 1-4392-2907-4
EAN13: 9781439229071

Visit www.booksurge.com to order additional copies.

CONTENTS

INTRODUCTION

What This Book Is About

There are several good books about software testing available. So why yet another? Over the course of several years, in my role as a Contributing Editor for Microsoft's MSDN Magazine I interviewed hundreds of software development managers and test managers. A nearly universal comment from these managers was something along the lines of, "When we hire new software test engineers they really have to learn on the job. We have books that describe software testing in a very general way, and we have books that provide detailed technical information about specific testing techniques, but what we don't have is a book that covers what we consider to be core software testing principles." I then started asking software testing managers what they thought these core software testing principles are. Not too surprisingly, there were many topics mentioned. However, certain testing topics seemed to appear over and over again in these conversations. The topics in this book are the topics that were mentioned most often by experienced software test engineers as being on their personal list of fundamental principles and essential knowledge for new testers.

In most computer science related books, the contents of the book are summarized in the introduction. I will forego that tradition and say instead that the best way to get a feel for what is covered in this book is to scan the table of contents; I know that's what I always do. That said however, let me mention a few topics that distinguish this book from other books on testing. Chapter 2, "Fundamental Mathematical Techniques", presents a concise summary of key mathematical skills needed in a software testing environment. In addition to basic combinatorics, including pair-wise testing, the chapter contains a quick overview of statistical and cryptographic techniques. Chapter 3, "Project Management Concepts", describes useful techniques for managing various aspects of a software testing effort, including time and cost estimation. Chapter 6, "Units, Modules, and Components", explains how to test the primary building blocks of modern software systems, including an explanation of the differences between unit testing and module testing.

The topics in this book were written so that they are independent from each other for the most part so that you can read them in any order. Each topic has a quick self-assessment question that is intended to reveal if you grasped the key point of the topic. These reviews questions are very similar to the questions you might encounter on a software testing certificate exam.

Who This Book Is For

This book is intended for anyone who wishes to gain a quick, practical working knowledge of fundamental software testing principles, including software developers, project and program managers, students, support engineers, and of course software test engineers. Although the topics in this book will help you understand software testing, like many professions you can really only learn testing by actually testing software. The information in this book will provide you with a conceptual framework that will help you understand how different testing concepts and techniques are related, and enable you to learn software testing on the job more efficiently. This book is not intended to be a technical recipe-style collection of specific testing techniques, and this book is not an attempt to identify a definitive body of knowledge for software testing.

Based on my interviews and surveys, many experienced test engineers believe that great software testers have something usually called the testing mentality. There is no solid definition or description or unanimous agreement of exactly what this testing mentality characteristic is, but great software testers tend to approach testing differently from great developers. One of the traits commonly associated with a great software tester is the drive to break software. In other words, software test engineers enjoy trying to find errors in software and get satisfaction when they uncover a serious bug in a system. A closely related trait is the enjoyment of analysis. Great testers seem to take pleasure in examining exactly how a software system works. Another common perception is that great software testers have a creative aspect to their personalities which helps them exercise a system under test in interesting and unusual ways. And finally, most great software testers seem to have the propensity to be very detailed oriented and very methodical. A software testing mentality plus knowledge of the topics in this book can help you on the path towards becoming a great tester

Acknowledgements

I wish to thank my corporate Vice Presidents at Volt Information Sciences, Inc., Christina Harris and Patrick Walker, for actively supporting the development of this book, as well as for their enthusiastic and ongoing belief in the importance of education in general. I'm grateful to the technical reviewers who did a great job of improving the overall quality of this book. The primary technical reviewers were Paul Pardi (Edenic Software) and Doug Walter (Microsoft). Technical and editorial reviewers were Eric Grudzien (Volt), Jim Suruda, and Hugh Timmons (Volt). My editor-in-chief at Microsoft's MSDN Magazine, Howard Dierking, has been a champion for advancing the state of software testing knowledge and my MSDN articles provided the conceptual foundation for many of the topics in this book. My staff at Volt, Shirley Lin, Stacey Anderson, and Lauren Opstad, supplied indispensible help in the production of this book.

Legal Note

The information in this book is intended to provide you with practical help in testing software. All information is provided without warranty of any kind. No part of this book may be reproduced, stored in or introduced into a retrieval system, or transmitted in any form or by any means (including electronic, mechanical, photocopying, recording, or otherwise), for any purpose without the express written permission of the publisher.

CHAPTER I
SOFTWARE TESTING AND TEST CASES

Software testing is the process of investigating the quality of a software system. The most common activity in software testing is sending input to the system under test and then examining the result to determine a pass or fail result. The seven topics in the chapter deal with test cases, the single most important entity for all software testing activities.

1.1 Test Cases

A test case normally consists of at least the following items: a test case ID, a test case input, and a test case expected result or state. For example, suppose a component under test is simply a function Sum (x, y) which accepts two integer arguments, x and y, and returns their sum. A test case always produces a result of either pass or fail. In situations where input is sent to a software system and there is no expected result, and therefore does not produce a pass or fail result, the process is more accurately called test analysis or test exploration rather than a executing a test case. Data for a single test case for Sum() might look like:

```
ID: 001
input1: 3
input2: 4
expected: 7
```

If the test case is intended to be executed by test automation through the use of a test harness program, the test case might be part of a data file of test cases along the lines of:

```
001:3:4:7
002:2:2:4
003:0:6:6
etc.
```

If the test case is intended to be executed manually, the test case might be part of a document which also contains a list of step-by-step instructions for performing the test:

"Launch the current build of the system. Enter "3" into the text box labeled "input1". Enter "4" . . . etc.

The sole purpose of a test case is to determine if there is an error of some sort in the system under test. In some academic circles the use of the term "bug" is frowned on, but it is commonly used in practice. Technically, terms such as anomaly, fault, error, failure, and defect are preferred by some academics but there is no consensus for the exact meanings of these terms. Therefore in practice the term bug has multiple meanings including an error in the source code of a system under development, and erroneous behavior of the SUD while executing.

Test case IDs are useful so that individual test cases can be combined into different collections called test suites. All test cases can be maintained in one central location and various test suites only need a list of the IDs of those test cases which make up each suite. Test case IDs are also useful to provide a reference to bugs which were found when the test case executed. For example, a bug tracking database can have a field in a bug report which holds the ID of the test case which revealed the bug.

Software utility programs called test case managers can be used to store and sometimes execute individual test cases. Test case managers can range from a simple spreadsheet file to sophisticated systems which not only store test case data, but also execute the test cases, store test case results, and maintain bug reports and other data.

In order for a test case to have an expected result or state, the system under test must start from some known state. For example, if you are testing the result of withdrawing money from a bank account, the expected result depends on the starting state of the account. Therefore, test case data must either assume some initial system state, or contain data to explicitly set the SUT to some state. Initialization data can range from simple, such as a single numeric value for a bank account module initial account balance, to complex, such as a large set of data for use in placing a SQL database into a known state. Similarly, determining the expected result or state of a SUT can range from simple, such as verifying a single numeric return value from a function, to complex, such as verifying the state of a database after some stored procedure has been executed.

The term test scenario is closely related to a test case and there is no clear distinction between the two. In general, a test case exercises the system under test to produce a single result or new state. A test scenario generally refers to situations where the SUT is manipulated through several state changes. For example, a test case might refer to a situation where a Web application is sent a single HTTP request, and the response stream is examined for an expected string of some sort. A test scenario might refer to a situation where a Web application is sent a series of inputs to generate a series of Web pages, and the final page is examined for an expected value. However, the distinction between test case and test scenario is arbitrary.

Review Question

Suppose you are testing a PinballMachine class which models a pinball machine and which is implemented using a language which supports object oriented programming (such as C#, C++, or Java). The PinballMachine class has a constructor which accepts a value representing an initial score, as well as Increase() and Decrease() methods which add points to and subtract points from a score member field of a PinballMachine object respectively. Which of the following sets of information best constitutes a reasonable test case?

a. { test case ID, constructor argument, one argument for the Decrease() method, one argument for the Increase() method }

b. { test case ID, constructor argument, two arguments for two calls to the Decrease() method, actual result value }

c. { test case ID, constructor argument, three arguments for three calls to the Decrease() method, expected result value }

d. { test case ID, constructor argument, comment }

1.2   Equivalence Classes

Equivalence class testing is a technique intended to reduce the number of test cases for a system under test without significantly reducing the effectiveness of the test effort. An equivalence class is a subset, or partition, of input values that are assumed to have roughly the same behavior in the sense that every value will either be handled correctly by the SUT or generate an error. Therefore instead of using every value in a particular class, you can just use one value from the class as test case input. The idea is best explained by example. Suppose you are testing some software application which deals with shipping weights. The logic in the application branches for weights between 0.1 lbs and 1.9 lbs. inclusive, weights between 2.0 lbs. and 9.9 lbs. inclusive, and weights greater than or equal to 10.0 lbs. This scenario creates the following four partitions for an input weight w : w < 0.1, 0.1 <= w <= 1.9, 2.0 <= w <= 9.9, and w >= 10.0. So instead of generating thousands of test cases for possible values of w, you can generate just four test cases, with each test case having an input value from one of the four equivalent partition classes. For example, the set { 0.0 lbs., 1.0 lbs., 5.0 lbs., and 100 lbs. } contains one input value from each of the four equivalence classes.

The principle of testing using equivalence classes does not mean you should only select one value from each partition. In general more test cases are better than fewer test cases. In practice, although the idea of equivalence class testing is simple, actually performing equivalence class testing can be quite difficult. There are two main problems. First, determining equivalent input classes is difficult even when you have access to the source code of the system under test. And if you do not have source code access you must rely on system specification documentation which may be incomplete, out of date, or simply non-existent. The second main problem with equivalence class testing is that it can be difficult to justify the underlying assumption that every input value from an equivalence class will behave the same.

Equivalence class testing is often best suited for use with software systems which have numeric inputs such as the example above, mostly because numeric data is more easily partitioned than string data. Equivalence class testing is closely related to boundary value testing. Because boundary values are those values which are exactly at, just above, and just below the defined limits of an input domain, when determining boundary values you are effectively determining partitions, some of which could be (but are not necessarily) equivalence classes. Additionally, the main purpose of equivalence class testing is to reduce the number of test case inputs in situations where the number of possible inputs is very large while the main purpose of boundary value testing is to explicitly test inputs which are likely to generate an error.

Review Question

Suppose you are testing some function which accepts the voltage of some electronic device as an input argument. The function performs internal branching logic depending on whether the voltage is "low" (0 through 10 volts), "medium" (11 through 19 volts), or "high" (20 volts and greater). Which of the following sets of test case input values best illustrates the concept of reducing the number of test cases by using equivalence classes?

a. { -10, 4, 16, 32 }
b. { 0, 10, 11, 19, 20 }
c. { 11, 13, 15, 17, 19 }
d. { 20, 30, 40, 50 }

1.3   Boundary Conditions

Testing boundary conditions in a system means testing those inputs which are exactly at, just above, and just below the defined limits of an input domain. In general, these boundary values are more likely to generate logic errors in a software system than arbitrary input values. Suppose you are testing a function Grade() which accepts an integer in the range [0..100] which represents a score on an exam, and which returns a letter grade that corresponds to the numeric score. For example, suppose scores of 90-100 are an "A", scores 80-89 are a "B", scores 70-79 are a "C", scores 60-69 are a "D", and scores 0-59 are an "F". In this situation the 22 boundary values are:

{ -1, 0, 1, 58, 59, 60, 61, 68, 69, 70, 71, 78, 79, 80, 81, 88, 89, 90, 91, 99, 100, 101 }

The example above is somewhat artificially simple. The real difficulty when testing with boundary values is determining exactly what the boundary values are. If the design of the system under test is thoroughly documented then you may be able to determine boundary values from the system specification documents. If the source code of the system under test is thoroughly commented and you access to the source code, you may be able to infer boundary values from the source code.

Boundary conditions can appear in a software system in a size context as well as a value context. For example, suppose some system under test defines an array of characters of size 256 along the lines of:

```
char[] buffer = new char[256];
```

Here you would want to create test case inputs which generate buffer sizes of -1, 0, 1, 255, 256, and 257 characters. Exactly how you would do this would depend on the details of the SUT. Or suppose a Web application defines an HTML text box along the lines of:

```
<input type="text" name="zip" size="5" maxlength=
"5" />
```

In terms of size, you would want to create test cases with inputs of length 0, 1, 4, 5, and 6. It is usually more difficult to determine boundary values when working with arbitrary non-numeric input such as strings than when working with numeric input. For example, suppose you are testing some function Reverse() which accepts an arbitrary string as an input parameter and which returns a string with the characters in reverse order. Without any additional information you cannot determine what reasonable boundary values are, although you could test input string size with strings of length 0, 1, maxLength-1, maxLength, and maxLength+1, where maxLength depends upon the programming environment. For example, the maximum size of a C# language string is 2,147,483,647 characters, and the maximum length of an Internet Explorer URL is 2,083 characters.

Review Question

Suppose you are testing some system which accepts arbitrary integer inputs. Which of the following sets of values best illustrates boundary condition test inputs?

a. { minint, -11,111, 1, maxint }
b. { minint, minint+1, -1, 0, 1, maxint-1, maxint }
c. { 0, 1, 4, 9, 16, 25, 36 }
d. { 0, 1, 2, 3, 5, 8, 13 }

1.4   Test Suites

A test suite is a collection of test cases. Different test suites are typically used for different purposes. Build Verification Tests (BVTs) are a suite of tests run just after a new build of the system under development has been created. The purpose of a BVT test run is to determine whether or not the new build of the system meets a set of minimal requirements so that software test engineers can effectively test the build and so that development engineers can effectively continue to add new features and fix existing bugs. BVTs often contain one or more test cases which verify that the system under test can be successfully installed — if the system under development cannot be installed than it is unlikely that any effective testing or development can be performed. BVTs often contain a set of basic functionality tests for the same reason. Test cases in a BVT suite are generally automated tests so that the BVT suite as a whole can be automated as part of the build process. If a new build of the system under development passes all tests in the BVT suite, then team members are notified that the build is released to test. If the new build fails one or more tests in the BVT suite, then team members typically receive a message that the build has failed the BVT.

Developer Regression Tests (DRTs) are a suite of tests run against new code before the new code is checked into a source code control repository. DRTs are sometimes performed by individual developers after they write new code, or sometimes performed as part of an automated source code check-in system. The larger and more complex the system under development is, the more likely it is that DRTs will be used as part of the development process.

A full test pass suite generally consists of every current test case. Full test pass suites are run before any milestone type of release of the system under development, such as a beta release, an agile iteration release, or a major milestone (MM) release. A full test pass is also run before the final release of a product. Final releases are sometimes called RTM (release to manufacturing in the case where the system is transferred to physical media such as a DVD disk), RTW (release to Web in the case where the system is made available as a download via the Internet), or RTO (release to operations in the case where the system is a Web application and is turned over to a group in charge of hosting the application on Web servers).

Depending on the scale and complexity of the system under development, and on the software development methodology being used, a test effort may use various test suites designed to be run at different times. Examples include daily test run suites, weekly test suites, and monthly test suites.

Review Question

Which of the following statements is most likely true about a Build Verification Test (BVT) suite?

a. BVTs are usually run before a new build of the system under development has been completed but after the build is released to test.

b. BVTs are usually run after a new build of the system under development has been completed but before the build is released to test.

c. BVTs are usually run by developers before new source code for the system under development has been checked into a source code repository tool.

d. BVTs are usually run by program management after the system under development has reached a milestone release.

1.5 Code Coverage

Code coverage is a metric used to measure how thoroughly a set of test cases exercises a software system. The basic idea of code coverage is best explained by example. Suppose you are testing some scientific library that performs various mathematical computations. The library contains 100 functions. You have a set of 1,000 test cases. When you run the set of 1,000 test cases you discover that 85 of the 100 functions in the library are called by at least one test case. Your code coverage metric for this example is 85% function coverage. This means that your set of test cases doesn't touch 15 of the 100 functions in the system under test so you need to create additional test cases. Code coverage, which measures test set thoroughness, is closely related to mutation testing, which measures test set effectiveness.

Code coverage can be difficult to perform because the source code of the system under test must be instrumented in some way to report when it is being touched by test code. In a complex software system this can be very challenging. In practice, rather than directly instrument the code of the system under test, code coverage usually works by taking an un-instrumented version of the system under test, using it as input to a profiling tool, which generates an instrumented version of the system which can then be tested and in turn generate code coverage metrics.

There are various levels of detail, or granularity, of code coverage. The least granular level of coverage is function coverage. This determines only if a function has been called by a test case. A more granular type of code coverage is basic block coverage where several related statements in the system under test are grouped as a block. Intermediate levels of granularity of code coverage include statement coverage (each individual statement in the system under test), decision coverage (each decision control structure, such as if.. then), and branch coverage (each true-false branch of each decision and loop control structure). The most detailed type of code coverage is full path coverage where every possible path of execution of the system under test is instrumented. Full path coverage is rarely possible in practice but may be required for the software of critical systems such as those used for medical devices or weapons control.

Although code coverage can reveal roughly how much of the system under test is exercised by a set of test cases, code coverage metrics do not directly indicate the quality of test cases.

Review Question

Which of the following code coverage metrics most likely indicates that the system under test has been most thoroughly tested by the associated test suite?

a. Test suite A with 60% statement coverage.
b. Test suite B with 80% statement coverage.
c. Test suite C with 60% function coverage.
d. Test suite D with 80% function coverage.

1.6 Mutation Testing

Mutation testing is a technique used to determine how well a set of test cases exercises a system under test. Mutation testing, which measures test set effectiveness, is closely related to code coverage, which measures test set thoroughness. Here's an example to illustrate the basic idea behind mutation testing. Suppose you are testing a cryptographic library of some sort which performs various types of data encryption and decryption. For simplicity, suppose that the library has exactly 100 functions, and each function has exactly 10 Boolean operators, such as if (x != 0) for example. So, there are a total of 100 * 10 = 1,000 Boolean operators in the library. Mutation testing works by mutating part of the system under test. In theory, if you mutate the system under test, presumably creating a logic error, and then execute a set of test cases, you should see at least one new test case failure indicating that a test case has caught the logic error. On the other hand, if you do not see a new test case failure, your existing set of test cases does not test for the logic error.

Continuing with the example above, mutation testing assumes that you have a set of test cases which do not generate any failures. Suppose you have 500 such test cases. Suppose the very first of the 1,000 total Boolean operators in the source code is:

```
if (n >= 0)
    // some code
```

You change the Boolean operator in the source code to its logical complement:

```
if (n < 0)
    // some code
```

Now you rebuild the system, and execute your 500 test cases which formerly did not yield any failures and you should now see at least one failure indicating at least one test case caught the bug introduced by the mutation. If you do not see any test case failures you would create a new test case that targets the mutated logic. Now you would go back to the source code, repair the first mutation with correct code and then mutate the second Boolean operator, and re-run your test suite. You would repeat this process with all 1,000 Boolean operators.

The example just described mutates Boolean operators by replacing each operator with its logical complement. It is possible to mutate other parts of the code of the system under test, such as mutating data. Mutation testing is challenging primarily because it requires a lot of time and effort. In practice, rather than try to mutate every Boolean operator in the system under test, software test engineers often use their background and experience to selectively target Boolean operators in the modules most likely to have logic errors.

Review Question

Which of the following mutation testing scenarios most likely suggests that the associated test suite covers the system under test most effectively?

a. Test suite A which initially yields 0 test case failures; 3,000 mutations which yield 500 additional test case failures.

b. Test suite B which initially yields 0 test case failures; 3,000 mutations which yield 400 additional test case failures.

c. Test suite C which initially yields 0 test case failures; 2,000 mutations which yield 30 additional test case failures.

d. Test suite D which initially yields 0 test case failures; 2,000 mutations which yield 10 additional test case failures.

1.7 Static Code Analysis

Static code analysis is the process of examining the source code or object code of the system under development, as opposed to examining the behavior of the SUD while the system is executing. There are many types of static code analysis. One of the oldest and most widely known types of static analysis is called cyclomatic complexity analysis. Cyclomatic complexity is a metric which is the number of independent execution paths through a software module. Cyclomatic complexity is based on graph theory where a program's control flow is modeled as a graph. Consider this artificially simple example:

```
int max(int a, int b)
{
  int answer;
  if (a > b)
    answer = a;
  else
    answer = b;
  return answer;
}
```

The cyclomatic complexity of this module is 3. There are two paths through the function, and by definition a return statement adds another path, for a total of three paths. In practice, cyclomatic complexity is usually determined by using a software tool rather than computed by hand. The basic principle of cyclomatic complexity is that more complex modules are more likely to contain logic errors than simple modules. For cyclomatic complexity, a general rule of thumb is that a module that has complexity higher than 10 should be examined to see if the module can be refactored into smaller, less complex modules. In some software development scenarios, a maximum complexity value is established. After each build, the modules of the SUD are examined using static code analysis techniques. If any module exceeds the established maximum complexity threshold value, the build as a whole fails the complexity test.

Cyclomatic complexity was devised in the 1970s before the widespread use of object oriented programming languages. OOP static analysis examines the structure of classes, methods, properties, and other features that are associated with OOP design. Examples of characteristics which could indicate an overly-complex design and therefore susceptibility to bugs include the number of data fields and methods in a class, the number of input parameters in a method, the number of static variables, the number of method calls made by a particular method, and so on. In some development scenarios, an OOP based static code analysis is performed on the system under development and any classes which have a high design complexity value are flagged for review and closer examination.

In a Microsoft .NET programming environment, FxCop is a standard static code analysis tool which primarily examines the SUD for usage patterns rather than complexity characteristics. It examines a system's .NET intermediate language code which is derived from the system's source code for a wide range of potentially error-prone patterns. Examples of usage warnings include, "Do not call overridable methods in constructors", "Collection properties should be read only", "Do not raise reserved exception types", and so on. Many other programming environments have similar tools. For example, in a Java programming environment the open source FindBugs tool examines bytecode for similar potential usage trouble spots.

Another type of static code analysis is dependency analysis. Dependency analysis examines the source code of a system to determine how many methods are called by a method in the system, and similarly, how many different methods call a particular method. The idea is that a method which has many calls to other methods may be overly complex and is more likely to contain bugs.

Review Question

Which of the following statements about cyclomatic complexity metrics is most often true?

a. Cyclomatic complexity metrics directly measure the CPU usage of a software system.

b. Cyclomatic complexity metrics directly measure the memory usage of data structures in a software system.

c. Cyclomatic complexity metrics directly measure the hard disk usage of a software system.

d. All of the above.

e. None of the above.

CHAPTER 2
FUNDAMENTAL MATHEMATICAL TECHNIQUES

Many software testing activities produce metrics. Therefore, software test engineers must have a basic understanding of the most common mathematical techniques used to analyze these metrics. The seven topics in this chapter describe basic statistical techniques, basic combinatorial techniques, and basic data encryption techniques which are commonly used in a software testing environment.

2.1 Measures of Central Tendency

Many areas of software testing involve metrics. The most fundamental descriptive statistic is the arithmetic mean, which is simply the normal average, or the sum of a set of values divided by the number of values in the set. The mode, the most common value in a set of values, and the median, the middle value (after sorting) of a set of values are also common measures of central tendency. There are two other types of means which are sometimes used in a software testing environment. The geometric mean is used when the values under consideration are ratios. The geometric mean of n values is computed as the nth root of the product of the values. For example, the (geometric) mean of the ratios 5:1, 4:1, and 2:1 is the cube root of 5 * 4 * 2 = 3.42:1. The harmonic mean is used when the values under consideration are rates. The harmonic mean is computed as the inverse of the sum of the arithmetic mean of the inverses of the values. For example, suppose a car travels a distance of 120 miles from point A to point B at a rate of 30 miles per hour. Then the car turns around and travels from point B to point A at a rate of 60 miles per hour. The average rate of speed is not (30 + 60) / 2 = 45.0 miles per hour, but rather 1 / ((1/30 + 1/60) / 2) = 40.0 miles per hour.

Pareto charts are often used in software testing environments. A Pareto chart is a bar graph where the categories on the x-axis are listed in descending order based on their associated counts or frequencies. A common use of Pareto charts is to visually display the frequencies of various categories of bugs. For example, suppose bugs in a bug tracking tool are categorized as setup bugs, performance bugs, functionality bugs, and accessibility bugs. Further, suppose there are 8 setup bugs, 6 performance bugs, 24 functionality bugs, and 12 accessibility bugs. A Pareto chart would display this information as a series of bars with functionality as the first category with a height of either 24 (counts) or 24 / 50 = 48% (frequency). Accessibility would be the second category, setup the third category, and performance as the fourth category. Pareto charts are a simple but effective way to visually emphasize the relative magnitudes of different category counts or frequencies.

A rare but dangerous statistical pitfall in a software testing environment is called Simpson's Paradox. The paradox is, briefly, a situation when two or more data sets evaluated individually lead to one conclusion, but the combined data set leads to an opposite conclusion. Here's an example. Suppose you have two different software system prototypes, Prototype A and Prototype B. You want to evaluate which prototype is better based on user feedback. Now suppose that for performance, Prototype A received an "excellent" evaluation by 50 out of 200 people, while Prototype B received "excellent" from 15 out of 100 people. So from this data, Prototype A is clearly superior to Prototype B for ease of use, with Prototype A getting 25% "excellent" and Prototype B getting just 15%. Furthermore suppose that for usability features, Prototype A receives an "excellent" rating from 85 out of 100 people, while Prototype B receives excellent from 300 out of 400 people. From this data, Prototype A (85% excellent) is again clearly superior to Prototype B (just 75% excellent). But suppose these two data sets are combined:

```
               Prototype A    Prototype B
Excellent:     135            315
Total:         300            500
Percent:       45%            63%
```

If you combine the number of "excellent" evaluations, you see that Prototype A receives 135 / 300 = 45% excellent, while Prototype B now dominates with 315 / 500 = 63% excellent! So, from combined data Prototype B is now rated significantly superior to Prototype A. This is a very strange effect. As it turns out, the initial uncombined data is correct and combining result data produced an incorrect evaluation in this example.

Review Question

Which of the following statements best describes the statistical measure of central tendency which should most often be used according to the type of data under consideration?

a. For ratio data the arithmetic mean should be used. For rate data, the mode should be used. For ordinary data the median should be used.

b. For ratio data the Chi-square mean should be used. For all other data the arithmetic mean should be used.

c. For ratio data the geometric mean should be used. For rate data, the harmonic mean should be used. For ordinary data the arithmetic mean, mode, or median should be used.

d. For ratio data the standard deviation should be used. For rate data, the variance should be used. For ordinary data the average absolute deviation should be used.

2.2 Measures of Variance

A statistical measure of variance or dispersion is a value that indicates how close the values in a set of numbers are to each other, or alternatively how far apart the values are. The three most common measures of dispersion used in software testing are the range, population variance, and population standard deviation. The range of a set of values is simply the high value minus the low value. So, suppose you are testing the performance of some software system and the results of five test runs are 3.0, 6.0, 8.0, 11.0, and 12.0 seconds. The range for this set of data is 12.0 - 3.0 = 9.0 seconds. Although the range can be useful, it is not a very sensitive metric. For example, suppose the performance results were 3.0, 3.0, 3.0, 3.0, and 12.0 seconds. The range is still 9.0 seconds but the data in the second set are clearly closer together than the data in the first set. Because of the relative lack of sensitivity of the range, the population variance and population standard deviation are used more often in software testing environments.

The population variance of a set of numbers is equal to the sum of squared differences from the mean, divided by the number of values. So for the example above where the data set is 3.0, 6.0, 8.0 11.0, 12.0, the mean equals 40.0 / 5 = 8.0 seconds. The sum of squared differences from the mean is: $(3.0 - 8.0)^2 + (6.0 - 8.0)^2 + (8.0 - 8.0)^2 + (11.0 - 8.0)^2 + (12.0 - 8.0)^2 = 5.0^2 + 2.0^2 + 0.0^2 + 3.0^2 + 4.0^2 = 54.0$. And so the population variance is 54.0 / 5 = 10.8 sec^2. Notice that because the population variance is computed as a sum of squared values, the result has units which are squared, in this case $seconds^2$. In most cases, such as this one, squared units such as sec^2 do not have any physical meaning; they are merely a mathematical consequence of how the variance is calculated.

Because of the awkwardness of the squared units of the variance, in most software testing situations the population standard deviation is used as a measure of dispersion rather than the variance. The standard deviation is simply the square root of the variance. So for the example above, the standard deviation is sqrt(10.8 sec^2) = 3.3 seconds. Notice that the square root operation causes the units of the standard deviation to be the same as the units of the original data.

In addition to the population variance and the population standard deviation, measures of dispersion, there are two variants called the sample variance and the sample standard deviation. These measures are used when you wish to infer the value of some global metric and your data is a randomly selected sample from a population of values which are distributed according to the Normal (bell curve) distribution. The sample variance is computed exactly as the population variance except that the sum of squared values is divided by the number of values minus 1. So for the example above, the sample variance is 54.0 / (5 - 1) = 13.5 sec^2. The sample standard deviation is the square root of the sample variance, or sqrt(13.5 sec^2) = 3.7 sec. Deciding whether to use the population standard deviation or the sample standard deviation is very subtle even for experts. As a general rule of thumb, in most software testing scenarios, the random selection and Normal distribution assumptions are hard to justify, so the population standard deviation is most often used. Whenever reporting standard deviation results, you should clearly state whether the population or sample standard deviation was used.

Review Question

Which of the following measures of dispersion is most often used in software testing scenarios?

a. The range.

b. The population variance.

c. The population standard deviation.

d. The sample variance.

e. The sample standard deviation.

2.3 Mathematical Permutations

A mathematical permutation is a rearrangement of a set of items. Permutations are important in several areas of software testing including configuration testing, module testing, and test case generation. The Factorial() function is used is compute the number of permutations there are for a given set of items. The definition of the Factorial() function is:

Factorial(n) = n * n-1 * n-2 * . . . * 1

The Factorial() function is often written using the '!' character, in other words as n! instead of Factorial(n). Suppose you have 4 items, { a, b, c, d }. The number of ways you can rearrange them is given by:

Factorial(4) = 4! = 4 * 3 * 2 * 1 = 24

The Factorial() function tells you how many permutations there are for a given number of items but the function does not tell you how to list them. For the set of four items above, the 24 different permutations are:

```
{a,b,c,d}
{a,b,d,c}
{a,c,b,d}
{a,c,d,b}
{a,d,b,c}
{a,d,c,b}
{b,a,c,d}
{b,a,d,c}
{b,c,a,d}
```

```
{b,c,d,a}
{b,d,a,c}
{b,d,c,a}
{c,a,b,d}
{c,a,d,b}
{c,b,a,d}
{c,b,d,a}
{c,d,a,b}
{c,d,b,a}
{d,a,b,c}
{d,a,c,b}
{d,b,a,c}
{d,b,c,a}
{d,c,a,b}
{d,c,b,a}
```

The number of permutations of a set of items starts out small for small values of n but becomes very, very large, very quickly. For example, the number of permutations of 10 items is Factorial(10) = 10! = $10 * 9 * 8 * 7 * 6 * 5 * 4 * 3 * 2 * 1$ = 3,628,800 which isn't too terribly large. But the number of permutations of 64 items is Factorial(64) = 64! = approximately 126,886,932,100,000,0 00,000,000,000,000,000,000,000,000,000,000,000,000,00 0,000,000,000,000,000 which is a number that is vastly, vastly larger than the estimated age of the universe measured in seconds. Because the Factorial() function can yield such large results, you should be careful about arithmetic overflow when calculating permutations.

Review Question

Suppose you are performing module testing on some method Foo() which has signature:

```
string Foo(string s1, string s2, string s3)
```

You wish to test all possible orders of inputs where s1, s2, and s3 take on the permutations of the values of "alpha", "beta", and "gamma". How many test cases will you generate for this scenario?

a. Factorial(3) = 3! = $3 * 3 * 3$ = 27

b. Factorial(3) = 3! = $3 * 2 * 1$ = 6

c. Factorial(9) = 9! = 9 * 9 = 81

d. Factorial(9) = 9! = (9 * 8) * (9 * 8) = 5,184

2.4 Mathematical Combinations

Combinatorics is a branch of mathematics that includes the study of the ways to select a subset of items from a larger set, and of the ways to rearrange a set of items. A mathematical combination is a subset of a larger set of items. A basic knowledge of combinatorics is essential for understanding many topics in software testing, including configuration testing, module testing, and test case generation. The combinatorial Choose(n,k) function can be used to determine the number of ways there are to select k items from a group of n items, where the order of the selected items is not relevant. One of several computational definitions of Choose(n,k) is:

Choose(n,k) = (n * n-1 * . . . * n-k+1) / (k * k-1 * . . . * 1)

For example, suppose you have a set of n = 6 items, {a, b, c, d, e, f}, and you wish to select 3 of them. The number of ways to do this is given by:

Choose(6,3) = (6 * 5 * 4) / (3 * 2 * 1) = 20

One way to view this formula is to remember that the result of Choose(n,k) is a fraction. On the bottom, denominator, place k numbers starting from k, and subtracting 1 each time, down to 1, and multiply. On the top, numerator, place k numbers, starting from n, and subtracting 1 each time, and multiply. There are several other formulas for the Choose() function, including formulas which use the Factorial() function. The Choose() function tells you how many ways there are to select a subset from a larger set, but there is no easy way to actually list the elements of the subset. In the example above, the 20 subsets are:

```
{a,b,c}
{a,b,d}
{a,b,e}
{a,b,f}
{a,c,d}
{a,c,e}
{a,c,f}
{a,d,e}
```

```
{a,d,f}
{a,e,f}
{b,c,d}
{b,c,e}
{b,c,f}
{b,d,e}
{b,d,f}
{b,e,f}
{c,d,e}
{c,d,f}
{c,e,f}
{d,e,f}
```

Notice that combination element {a,b,c} is listed but element {c,b,a} is not listed because it is assumed that order does not matter when using the Choose() function. If order does matter when calculating the number of subsets of a larger set, you simply multiple the result of the Choose(n,k) function by k! because each subset of size k can be rearranged in k! ways. For the example above, notice that the first subset {a,b,c} has 3! = 6 permutations. Therefore the total number of ways to select 3 items from a group of 6 items where order matters is Choose(6,3) * 3! = 20 * 6 = 120.

Review Question

Suppose you are testing some system which involves a normal 52-card deck of cards. Which of the following represents the number of ways you can select 4 cards from the deck, without replacement, where the order of the selected cards does not matter?

a. Choose(52,4) = (52 * 52) * (4 * 4)

b. Choose(52,4) = (52 * 51 * 50 * 49 * 4 * 3 * 2 * 1)

c. Choose(52,4) = (52 * 51 * 50 * 49) / (4 * 3 * 2 * 1)

d. Choose(52,4) = (52 * 52 * 52 * 52)

2.5 Data Encryption

Data encryption is the process of scrambling data so that unauthorized users cannot interpret the data. Data decryption is the process of unscrambling encrypted data. Before encrypting, data is usually called plain text. After encryption the data is usually called cipher text. In informal usage, the terms encoding and decoding are sometimes used instead of encryption and decryption. A fundamental knowledge of encryption is required for many areas of security testing.

There are two broad categories of encryption: symmetric key encryption and public key encryption. Symmetric key encryption uses a single key which is used to both encrypt and decrypt data. Here is an example of symmetric key encryption using a hypothetical language:

```
SymmetricCryptoObject des = new
 SymmetricCryptoObject("DES");
byte[] key = StringToKey("Secret");
string plainText = "A sensitive message";
byte[] ciphertext = des.Encrypt(plainText, key);
byte[] decodedText = des.Decrypt(cipherText, key);
```

There are many different symmetric key encryption algorithms. The example above uses the Digital Encryption Standard (DES) algorithm. Other common algorithms are Triple DES (a variation of DES), and the Advanced Encryption Standard (AES). The main point is that there is a single key value which both encodes and decodes data.

Public key encryption uses one key to encrypt data and a second, mathematically related key for decryption. For example:

```
PublicKeyCryptoObject rsa = new
 PublicKeyCryptoObject("RSA");
byte[] publicKey;
byte[] privateKey;
rsa.MakeUniqueKeyPair(publicKey, privateKey);
string plainText = "A sensitive message";
byte[] cipherText = rsa.Encrypt(plainText,
 publicKey);

byte[] decodedText = rsa.Decrypt(cipherText,
 privateKey);
```

Some common public key encryption algorithms are RSA (as in the hypothetical example above), DSA, and a class of algorithms called elliptic curve cryptography.

Most forms of symmetric key encryption and public key encryption are called block encryption algorithms because they operate on some fixed number of bytes. For example, the AES symmetric key algorithm encrypts data in blocks of size 128 bits = 16 bytes. Most data which is encrypted is much longer than the block size, so the data to be encrypted is broken down into smaller blocks. However, each block is not encoded in exactly the same way because anyone who intercepted the encrypted data blocks could infer the key by analyzing the frequency of encrypted bytes. For example, the most common byte sequence would likely represent character 'e' in normal English text. Therefore, the key for each block is modified using what is essentially a secondary key called an initialization vector.

Sometimes symmetric key and public key encryption are used together. Suppose Person A wishes to send Person B a sensitive message via e-mail. Person A cannot simply send Person B a symmetric key because A's e-mail could easily be intercepted. This is called the key exchange problem. Instead, Person A sends Person B an ordinary e-mail message, telling B that A wants to send B a sensitive message. Person B then generates a public key - private key pair, and sends only the public key via e-mail back to Person A. Because the public key is used only for encryption, even if Person B's message is intercepted, it would do the interceptor no good. Now person A generates a symmetric key and encrypts the symmetric key using the public key sent by Person B. Person A sends the public key encrypted symmetric key to Person B. Even if the encrypted key is intercepted, only B has the private key which can decrypt. Now B decrypts the symmetric key using the private key only B has. At this point both A and B have the same symmetric key (solving the key exchange problem). Person A now encrypts the sensitive message using the symmetric key, sends the encrypted message to Person B, who then decrypts the message using the same symmetric key.

Review Question

Which of the following statements about RSA public key encryption is true?

a. The plain text is encoded using a public key, and the resulting cipher text is decoded using an associated private key.

b. The plain text is encoded using a private key, and the resulting cipher text is decoded using an associated public key.

c. Both the plain text and resulting cipher text are encoded and decoded using the same symmetric key.

d. The plain text is encoded using a public key, but the resulting cipher text cannot be decoded except by brute force trial and error.

2.6 Crypto-Hashing

In software development and testing, the term hashing can have two closely related but functionally slightly different meanings. One use of the term hashing refers to using a type of function, called a hash function, to generate an integer value which acts as an ID of sorts for an object. The integer ID is then used as an index value to store the object into a data structure called a hash table. Hash table collections are used when a very quick search is needed. The second use of the term hashing refers to using a type of function, often called a crypto-hash, to generate a sequence of bytes which acts as an ID for an object for comparison purposes. There are several different types of crypto-hash algorithms. Two common crypto-hashes are MD5 (message digest version 5), and the newer SHA-1 (secure hash algorithm version 1).

Crypto-hash functions accept a sequence of bytes of any length and so can be used to compute an ID for any type of object including an image, the entire contents of a text file, a single integer, an object stored in memory, and so on. The result of a crypto-hash ID value is always a fixed size regardless of the size of the original input. The result of an MD5 hash is always exactly 16 bytes, and the result of an SHA-1 hash is always 20 bytes. For example, the MD5 crypto-hash value of the bytes represented by the entire Gettysburg Address speech (as a Unicode string) is D4-1D-8C-D9-8F-00-B2-04-E9-80-09-98-EC-F8-42-7E. One way to think of crypto-hashes is to consider them as one-way encryption. Even though crypto-hash algorithms are deterministic, they are very cleverly designed so that if you have a crypto-hash ID value, there is no practical way to determine the value of the original object. In other words there is no practical way to determine the original value for a sequence of bytes whose MD5 hash value is B6-65-D8-26-E9-19-38-10-52-EC-23-B9-EA-EC-3B-62.

One example of the use of crypto-hashes is as follows. A developer creates some code and makes this code available as a download via the Internet. The developer computes a crypto-hash of the code and published the value of the crypto-hash on the Web site that contains the link to the code download. Now when someone downloads the source code to a local computer, after the download is complete, the recipient uses the same crypto-hash algorithm to compute the crypto-hash of the downloaded file. If the resulting crypto-hash value matches the value published on the download Web site, then the downloader knows that the downloaded code is the same as the original code and has not been corrupted either accidentally or maliciously during transmission.

In software testing crypto-hash values are sometimes used to represent expected states for software test cases. For example, suppose you are testing a SQL stored procedure which inserts data into a SQL database. The actual state after calling the stored procedure under test will consist of all the data in all the tables in the database. Rather than storing this large amount of data as the expected state, just the crypto-hash ID of the data can be stored and used to represent the expected state.

Review Question

Which of the following statements about SHA-1 (Secure Hash Algorithm version 1) crypto-hashing is true?

a. The size of the output (in bytes) is always greater than or equal to the size of the input (in bytes).

b. The size of the output (in bytes) is always less than or equal to the size of the input (in bytes).

c. The size of the output is always 20 bytes regardless of the size of the input.

d. SHA-1 crypto-hashing is currently considered significantly less secure than MD5 crypto-hashing.

2.7 Pair-Wise Testing

Pair-wise testing is a technique used to reduce the number of test case inputs in situations where there are too many inputs to deal with. Suppose some system has three different input parameters, A, B, C. For example, if the system is a Web page, parameter A might be a drop down list, parameter B might be a set of radio buttons, and parameter C might be a check box. Suppose that parameter A can take on one of three possible values: red, blue, green. Suppose that parameter B can take on one of four possible values: alpha, beta, gamma, and delta. Suppose that parameter C can take on one of two values: true or false. In this situation there are a total of 3 * 4 * 2 = 24 possible test case inputs:

{ red, alpha, true }

{ red, alpha, false }

{ red, beta, true }

{ red, beta, false }

{ red, gamma, true }

{ red, gamma, false }

{ red, delta, true }

{ red, delta, false }

{ blue, alpha, true }

{ blue, alpha, false }

. . . etc . . .

{ green, delta, false }.

This is probably not too many test cases to test completely (unless the test cases are very costly or time consuming) and so you normally wouldn't use pair-wise testing for this example. But if you did use pair-wise testing the idea is to create a set of test case inputs which contain all possible pairs of inputs from each parameter. There is no easy way to compute how many pairs of inputs must be captured for a given problem. For this example there are 26 such pairs that must be captured by your test cases:

(red,alpha), (red,beta), (red,gamma), (red,delta), (red,true), (red,false), (blue,alpha), (blue,beta), (blue,gamma), (blue,delta), (blue,true), (blue,false),(green,alpha), (green,beta), (green,gamma), (green,delta), (green,true), (green,false), (alpha,true), (alpha,false), (beta,true), (beta,false), (gamma,true), (gamma,false), (delta,true), (delta,false).

Consider the test case { red, alpha, true }. It captures 3 of the 26 pairs: (red,alpha), (red,true), (alpha,true). So just how do you generate a set of test cases which capture all possible pairs? It turns out to be a very difficult problem (called an NP-complete problem) and in practice you need a tool to generate pair-wise test sets. One such tool is called PICT. PICT is available as a free download. The PICT tool generates 12 test cases for the example above:

{ green, alpha, true }

{ red, delta, true }

{ red, gamma, false }

{ blue, delta, false }

{ blue, gamma, true }

{ blue, alpha, false }

{ red, alpha, false }

{ green, beta, false }

{ blue, beta, true }

{ green, delta, true }

{ green, gamma, false }

{ red, beta, true }

These 12 test case inputs account for all 26 pairs. So, the pair-wise testing approach has reduced the number of test cases from 24 down to 12. The saving isn't considerable with this small dummy example but in a realistic example the reduction in number of test cases can be very significant. The idea behind pair-wise testing is the theory that logic errors in code are more likely to occur where values from different parameters interact than where values from a single parameter interact.

Review Question

Suppose you wish to use the pair-wise testing technique on a system which has three input parameters, A, B, and C. Parameter A accepts one of four values, a, b, c, d. Parameter B accepts one of two values, e, f. Parameter C accepts one of three values, g, h, i.

How many total pairs of input values must be captured by your set of test cases for this scenario?

a. 36 pairs.

b. 26 pairs.

c. 81 pairs.

d. 45 pairs.

CHAPTER 3
PROJECT MANAGEMENT CONCEPTS

The more complex a software testing effort is, the more likely it is that standard project management techniques will be useful to help the effort succeed. The seven topics in this chapter describe various project management principles and approaches which are useful in a software testing environment.

3.1 The Software Development Life Cycle

The software development lifecycle (SDLC) is a general term that refers to the overall process of creating a software system. There are several common categories of SDLC methodologies and many, many variations on each category. From a software testing perspective it is useful to categorize the type of SDLC methodology being used in a particular project, because different testing strategies and techniques are generally better suited for different types of methodologies.

The waterfall model is one of the oldest SDLC methodologies. The development process is organized into five distinct phases: requirements, design, implementation/coding, verification/testing, and release/maintenance. In the requirements phase, a highly detailed description of the system's goals is specified. The design phase results in a set of documents which describe the architectural details of the system. In the implementation phase, the system is actually coded by developers. The system is thoroughly tested in the verification phase. In the maintenance phase, the system under test is deployed and integrated with existing systems if necessary. In the waterfall model, each of the five phases is performed sequentially. The waterfall model tends to be well suited for software systems where requirements will not change during the development process, such as medical systems and weapons systems. In general, testing activities in a project which uses the waterfall methodology are highly structured, emphasizing the use of formal specification documents, detailed reporting, and traditional project management principles.

The spiral model is similar to the waterfall model in that there are a set of five general phases — requirements, design,

implementation/coding, verification/testing, and release/mainte-
nance — however each set of these five phases is repeated several
times. At the end of each cycle, a preliminary version of the system
has been produced. Then the overall system requirements and design are revised to take into account experience gained. The final
version of the system is typically released after three to five cycles
through the requirements-through-release process. Each cycle of
five phases takes roughly three to six months in many development
scenarios. Software testing activities on a spiral model project are
generally somewhat less formal than those on a waterfall model.

A relatively new variation of SDLC model called agile development
became popular starting in the mid 2000s. Agile development can
be thought of as an accelerated form of the spiral model. Again,
the requirements, design, implementation/coding, verification/
testing, release/maintenance activities are performed iteratively;
however each iteration typically takes only two to four weeks. As
with the waterfall and spiral models, there are countless variations
on the agile theme. Some of the characteristics often associated
with agile development are minimal reliance on formal written
documentation, early and extensive customer feedback, test driven
development (performing coding and testing simultaneously), and
pair programming (developers always working in pairs). Scrum is
a term which describes an approach to managing projects being
developed using agile methodologies.

Two closely related forms of SDLC methodology called the Personal Software Process (PSP) and the Team Software Process (TSP)
were developed in the mid 1990s. PSP/TSP is closely associated
with the Capability Maturity Model (CMM) which is a highly structured set of guidelines for measuring the progress of the business
processes associated with a software development project. CMM is
in turn closely associated with the Software Engineering Institute
(SEI), a hybrid federal-private organization which attempts to de-
fine software development best practices. PSP/TSP is an extremely
structured approach characterized by large numbers of project
managers, extensive use of form templates, and frequent review
meetings.

Many product groups at Microsoft use a SDLC methodology which
is sometimes called the synchronize and stabilize model, or simply

the Microsoft model. A primary characteristic of the Microsoft model is the production of a daily build of the system under development. Like the spiral model, the requirements through release set of activities are performed repeatedly. Phases of development have names such as minor milestone (mm), major milestone (MM), Alpha release, Beta release, and community technical preview (CTP). The final release activity is often called RTM (release to manufacturing), RTW (release to Web), or RTO (release to operations). The Microsoft SDLC model often uses dedicated software test engineers who work throughout the development process. There is often extensive use of both manual testing, generally performed by Software Test Engineers (STEs), and custom software test automation, generally written by Software Development/Design Engineers in Test (SDETs).

Review Question

Which of the following software development methodologies is least likely to be characterized by a test team which uses formal documentation and traditional project management techniques?

a. A variation of the waterfall software development methodology paradigm.

b. A variation of the spiral software development methodology paradigm.

c. A variation of the agile software development methodology paradigm.

d. A variation of the synchronize and stabilize software development methodology paradigm.

3.2 Project Management Constraints

In standard project management terminology, a project is an undertaking with defined start and finish dates that create a unique product or service. Many software development efforts as a whole, as well as software test efforts, fall into this definition. Arguably the most fundamental concept in project management is a principle known by various terms including the project management triple constraints, and the project management triangle. The three components of the project management triple constraints are time, scope, and budget. Time is a limitation for projects because by the very definition of a project there is a defined start and finish dates. Scope is the set of features which are to be included in the project. Budget is the amount of money allocated to the project. These three constraints are sometimes called by various aliases, such as schedule or duration for the time constraint, features for the scope constraint, and cost or money for the budget constraint. Somewhat curiously, quality is clearly a project constraint and is generally, but somewhat artificially, considered a part of the scope constraint. Quality is sometimes considered a fourth, separate but hidden member of the triple constraints.

The key idea behind the project management triple constraints is that a change in any one of the constraints will result in a change in one or both of the other two constraints (or other three constraints if you consider quality a separate constraint). For example, if the budget for a project is cut, then either the time required to finish the project will become longer (for example if the project substitutes lower cost employees who work slower than the higher cost employees originally budgeted), or the scope of the project will need to be reduced (for example by eliminating some features), or the quality of the project will need to be lowered (for example by reducing the amount of testing performed), or some combination of these effects. So for example, from the point of view of a software development project as a whole, if the overall software effort budget is cut, or if the time allowed for the development effort is shortened, or if the number of features in the system under development is increased, then the quality of the system under development will necessarily be reduced according to the project management triple constraints principle. Similarly, if just the software testing effort is considered a sub-project within the larger overall development project, then any change in the test effort budget, time, scope, or quality will affect one or more of the other constraints.

Review Question

Which of the following statements is true about the project management triple constraints?

a. Quality is often considered part of the time constraint.

b. Quality is often considered part of the budget constraint.

c. Quality is often considered part of the scope constraint.

d. Quality is not considered a project management constraint.

3.3 Beta Distribution Estimation

An important skill for testers is the ability to estimate how long a testing related task will require. One common technique is to use the mathematical Beta distribution. The first step is to break the overall task into smaller, more manageable sized chunks if necessary. At a coarse level of granularity tasks can be milestones (typically measured in weeks or months), or at a fine level of granularity these tasks can be work packages (typically lasting from 4 to 40 hours) that are derived from a project management Work Breakdown Structure. In general, time estimates for smaller tasks will be more accurate than time estimates for longer tasks.

Although it is possible to make a single, point estimate of how long the testing task under consideration will take, a better approach is to use the Beta distribution. To use the Beta distribution the tester determines three estimates of how long the task will require: an optimistic estimate, a pessimistic estimate, and a most likely case estimate. Of course this is the hard part, and testers must rely on historical data from similar projects, expert judgment, or some other method. Now the tester computes the duration mean and variance using the Beta distribution. The mean for a Beta distribution is the value (optimistic, plus 4 times most likely, plus pessimistic), divided by 6. For example, suppose the optimistic, pessimistic, and most likely estimates for some task are 5.0 days, 17.0 days, and 8.0 days respectively. The Beta average is (5.0 + 4 * 8.0 + 17.0) / 6 = 9.0 days. This overall time estimate for the task, along with the component optimistic, pessimistic, and most likely case estimates, can be reported which provides more information than a point estimate.

The Beta distribution can be used to optionally provide a rough so-called confidence interval time estimate. First the statistical variance is computed as the square of the quantity of the difference between the pessimistic and optimistic estimates, divided by 6. For the example above this is $((17.0 - 5.0) / 6)^2 = 4.00$ days^2. Next the standard deviation is computed as the square root of the variance, in this example, sqrt(4.00 days^2) = 2.00 days. The standard deviation can be used to compute an 80% confidence interval estimate by multiplying the standard deviation times the statistical Z-value for an 80% interval, which is 1.28. (Other intervals can be used too, but 80% is often a reasonable choice in software testing scenarios). So for this example the confidence interval time estimate for the task is:

= 9.0 days ± 1.28 * 2.00 days

= 9.0 days ± 2.56 days

And now the time estimate can be reported along the lines of, "Using an 80% statistical confidence level, the estimated time to complete (the task) is 9.0 days ± 2.56 days, or in other words between 6.44 days and 11.56 days." As with any quantitative technique, the final overall time Beta estimate is only as good as the initial three estimates.

Review Question

Suppose you are testing some system and your management has asked you to report how long it will take you to construct a set of manual test cases for a particular scenario. Which of the following approaches is most likely the best way to proceed?

a. Respond that time estimation is strictly a project/program management task and do not report any value.

b. Determine a single point estimate and report that value.

c. Determine optimistic, pessimistic, and most likely case estimates and report all three values.

d. Determine optimistic, pessimistic, and most likely case estimates, then use the Beta distribution to compute an overall estimate, and report all four values.

3.4 Test Effort Documentation

An effective software testing effort requires some form of coherent planning and reporting. There are several industry standard sets of guidelines and templates you can use when creating documentation for a software testing effort. One of the most important and widely referenced sets of standards is the IEEE 829 Standard for Software Test Documentation. The IEEE 829 standard is generic and does not provide specific guidelines for creating each document. The standard suggests that you create some or all of these four planning and four reporting documents:

1. Test Plan: relatively high level details of the test effort, including personnel, time estimates, scope of testing, and test host configurations.

2. Test Design Specification: rather high-level information about test case data such as the general forms of input values and expected results.

3. Test Case Specification: specific information about test case data such as specific test case input and expected values.

4. Test Procedure Specification: details of exactly how to execute each test case, such as any set-up preconditions and the manual steps.

5. Test Item Transmittal Report: details of how a test effort knows when the software system under development is ready to be tested.

6. Test Log: details of which tests cases were run, when they were run, and a pass / fail result.

7. Test Incident Report: information about test cases which failed for reasons such as an incorrect expected value or invalid configuration.

8. Test Summary Report: a complete summary of all tests executed, including details about whether exit criteria have been met or not.

The level of detail required in software testing documentation varies according to many factors. When testing the software for a critical system such as medical device, a high level of detail is required. When testing an application being developed using an agile methodology, less detail is required.

Another set of guidelines related to software testing documentation is the ISO (International Standards Organization) 9000-3 standards. ISO 9000-3 can be thought of as a lengthy checklist of items that should be performed. Examples include, "Develop documents that describe your life cycle models" and "Identify software product quality objectives and requirements." In addition to the generic IEEE 829 and ISO 9000-3 standards, specific test documentation templates are widely available on the Internet.

Review Question

In informal terms, information about a failed test case is often called a bug report. If you were following the IEEE 829 guidelines for software test documents, in which of the following documents would you most likely place your bug reports?

a. Test Plan.

b. Test Design Specification.

c. Test Procedure Specification.

d. Test Log

e. None of the above.

3.5 Source and Version Control Tools

A source control tool stores and manages the source code for a software system during the development process. Source control tools keep a copy of every version of the source code which is created and so are sometimes called version control tools. Simple source/version control tools use a locked check-in and check-out model. With this type of tool a developer checks code out from the source control database which copies the source code to the local development machine and which locks other developers from checking the same code out (although other developers may still examine the checked out code in read-only mode). After the developer makes changes to the source code, the new version of the code is checked back into the tool, and the old version is unlocked. More sophisticated source/version control tools allow multiple developers to check out the same code simultaneously, work on their own local versions independently, and then merge and store the multiple changes into a single new version. Additionally, sophisticated tools allow branching so that separate paths of development can be broken off from a common code base.

In many development scenarios, software test engineers must have a basic working knowledge of the source/version control tool being used on their project in order to be able to access the most current version of the system under development and test it. However in some development environments, a dedicated build team creates an installable version of the system under development from the code in the source control tool and then places the resulting system into a so-called drop point (typically a network share) where test engineers can copy the system to test host machines.

One of the oldest and most often used source/version control tools is CVS (Concurrent Versions System). CVS was originally created for use on Unix systems and is an open source tool. CVS is an adaptation of an even older source/version control tool called RCS (Revision Control System). CVS is a command line tool. If an engineer issues the command:

```
% cvs checkout myProject
```

then all of the files (such as main.c and myModule.c for example) in a project called myProject will be copied to the local host machine. After making edits, a command such as:

```
% cvs commit myModule.c
```

would check in edited file myModule.c back into the CVS data store. CVS is considered somewhat tricky to use. An open source tool called Subversion is a de facto successor to CVS. The Microsoft Corporation uses a proprietary source/version control tool called Source Depot. Source Depot was created to be able to handle huge projects with thousands of files and millions of lines of code. The predecessor of Source Depot was another Microsoft proprietary tool called SLM (Source Library Manager). Source Depot is a command line tool. Here are some example Source Depot commands:

```
C:\> sd sync
C:\> sd edit myModule.cs
C:\> sd submit
```

These commands first check out all files changed since the last sync command and copies those files to the local host machine, then enables editing of file myModule.cs, and then checks in all changes made back to the data store and saves them as a new version of the project under development. Because command line source/version control tools can be difficult to work with, several GUI based wrapper tools have been created for CVS and Source Depot.

In addition to specialized source/version control tools which are specifically designed for use with source code files, there are many tools which are more general purpose in nature and which can be used to manage any types of files such as word processing documents, PowerPoint files, spreadsheet files, and so on. An alternative to the use of dedicated source/version control tools is the use of tools which are integrated into development environment tools. One such example is the Team System for Microsoft Visual Studio.

Review Question

Which of the following statements is most often true of sophisticated source/version control repository tools such as CVS (Concurrent Versions System), Subversion, and Source Depot?

a. Version control tools usually store all old versions of the source code of the system under development and test, as well as the most recent version of source code.

b. Version control tools usually allow branching of source code which permits separate paths of development.

c. Version control tools usually allow merging of two or more separate paths of development into a single path of development.

d. All of the above.

e. None of the above.

3.6 Bug Reports

Most bug reporting tools provide you with an entry form which contains fields where you can select one of a list of values. Examples of such fields are severity, priority, assigned-to, area/category, configuration, and status. The values for some discrete fields in a bug report, such as date-entered, bug ID, and entered-by, are usually supplied automatically by bug reporting tools.

Bug severity is typically a numeric value between 1 and 4. In most cases severity = 1 indicates a crashing or hanging bug, or a bug where major functionality of the system under test is broken. Severity = 4 usually indicates a very minor bug, such as a misspelling in product documentation. Bug priority is also usually a value between 1 and 4 indicating how quickly the bug should be fixed. Priority 1 means the bug should be fixed as soon as possible; priority 4 is a very low priority bug. In many situations a bug is assigned severity and priority values which are the same. The most common exception to this rule of thumb is that a bug may be assigned a higher priority value than a severity value. This happens when the bug, even though not too severe in terms of system functionality, is a blocking issue and prevents testing or development progress. Additionally, a bug priority value is often increased as the system release date is approached.

The use of an assigned-to field in a bug report varies from test scenario to scenario. In situations where there is an independent test team with highly skilled test engineers, test engineers will directly assign a bug to a development engineer. In situations where testing is outsourced or with a non-integrated, relatively weak test team, test engineers may be required to leave the value of the assigned-to field as unassigned and let program management assign the bug to an appropriate developer.

Many bug report forms have a field which indicates a particular area or category of bug. Some common generic categories include: accessibility, basic functionality, code coverage, help, documentation, localization, load, stress, module, performance, security, setup, stability, user interface, usability, and printer. A category field may also be more specific to a system under development.

In many situations a configuration field value or set of values is included in a bug report. Configuration information often includes values such as test host operating system, internal memory, and processor type. More specific configuration information that is pertinent to a particular bug is typically included in the bug's reproduction steps. For example, a performance bug may be related to or dependent upon some other process or program running on the test host machine at the same time as test case execution.

In many situations there is a relation between a bug and one of more test cases. The ID of the test case or cases which result in a bug are often included in a bug report, or more rarely the ID of a bug may be stored as part of test case data. In some situations, such as a bug found by a beta user or through ad hoc testing, a bug will not have an associated test case.

Review Question

Which of the following combinations of severity and priority values are you least likely to see in a bug tracking database?

a. A bug with severity = 1 and priority = 1.

b. A bug with severity = 4 and priority = 4.

c. A bug with severity = 1 and priority = 4.

d. A bug with severity = 4 and priority = 1.

3.7 Reproduction Steps

The ability to communicate effectively is an essential skill for all software testers. A particularly important communication skill is writing clear, precise, and accurate bug reports. Bug report fields fall into two different categories: fields which have a list of discrete values to choose from (such as severity, functional area, person assigned to, and so on) in controls such as dropdowns and radio buttons, and text fields which accept free form input (such as title, description, reproduction steps, and comments). The first entry in a bug report is generally the bug title. A misspelled word in a bug report title can easily lead to duplicate bugs because the title and description fields are often the fields searched before entering a new bug in order to avoid a duplicate entry. The exact structure of a bug report title varies from effort to effort, and depends to a certain extent upon which bug tracking tool is used, but you should establish a consistent title scheme. For example, you may wish to precede every title with a product name and a test area:

Monad: Performance: Startup Time Too Long

The choice of a particular title scheme will depend greatly on your particular testing environment, but regardless of scheme it is important to be consistent. In general, bug reports contain a description field. A bug description is essentially an expanded title and gives team members additional information about the bug. A very general rule of thumb is that a bug description is often about three sentences in length. Again, correct spelling is important to avoid duplicate bugs.

The ability to write good repro (reproduction) steps is a skill that often distinguishes experienced testers from beginning testers. One of the main difficulties when writing repro steps is determining how detailed to make the steps. The level of detail in repro steps depends on many factors. For example, in an open source effort where there may be dozens of developers and testers who are widely distributed, and where team members frequently join and leave the effort, the repro steps in a bug will likely have to be quite detailed because you cannot assume team members have a great deal of context information. On the other hand, in a development effort with a small, stable team, the number of repro steps can be smaller. For example, the very first step in a set of repro steps might be something like, "Install build 2010.09.23.01". In some scenarios, every team member will know exactly how the build process works, where the build drop points are, and how to install a new build. However in other scenarios this type of information may need to be included in the repro steps. As a very general rule of thumb, in most standard development environments, the number of repro steps is typically about 4 to 20 — fewer steps likely do not provide enough detail but more steps likely are overkill.

Many bug report tools provide a comment field. Ultimately the purpose of a bug report is to provide enough information to developers so that the bug can be efficiently prioritized and fixed. The comment field can be used by experienced test engineers to help developers. For example, a test engineer may have a hunch of the cause of a bug and include that hunch in the comment field.

Review Question

When writing a bug report which of the following statements is most likely to be true?

a. The title field is generally longer than the description field.

b. The description field is generally longer than the title field.

c. A spelling error in the title field is usually less serious than a spelling error in the reproduction steps field.

d. A spelling error in the comments field is usually more serious than a spelling error in the description field.

CHAPTER 4
CORE PRINCIPLES

Surveys of hundreds of software test managers and software development managers consistently identified a core set of seven testing principles. The seven topics in this chapter describe the seven principles that emerged from these surveys. In general, these topics are not specific techniques, however understanding these principles is necessary in order to efficiently learn how to perform specific testing techniques associated with each principle.

4.1 Black Box and White Box Testing

Black box testing and white box testing are two common terms associated with software testing. In brief, black box testing refers to any type of testing which occurs when the software tester does not have detailed knowledge of the internal structure of the system under test. There are various degrees of black box testing. For example, a tester may not have access to the source code of the system under test but may have a specification document which details the data structures and algorithms used in the SUT, and another specification document which describes the SUT's functionality. In an extreme black box testing situation, the software tester may have no knowledge of the SUT at all. Although black box testing refers to any type of testing, in most situations black box testing encompasses functionality testing activities.

White box testing is a term that refers to any type of testing which occurs when the software tester has access to the internal structure of the system under test. There are various degrees of white box testing. For example, a tester may have access to the source code of certain modules which make up the system under test, but not have access to the source code of other modules in the SUT. In most situations, in order to thoroughly test a software system both black box and white box testing activities should be used.

In general, more information is better than less information, so why should a test effort employ black box testing? In some situations, software test engineers may not be granted access to the internal structure and source code of the system under test for contractual reasons. This can occur when the testing effort is outsourced and the company which is producing the software system being tested does not wish proprietary code to be exposed. In other situations, the test manager may intentionally withhold access to the source code of the SUT temporarily so that test engineers focus strictly on testing those aspects of the SUT which are defined in various specification documents.

The terms black box testing and white box testing are sometimes used to imply the coding skill required by a software test engineer. If a tester is using white box techniques, presumably the tester is examining the source code of the system under test which implies that the tester has the ability to understand code, which in turn implies that the tester has the ability to write code. Because software test engineers who can code are generally perceived as being higher skilled than test engineers who lack coding ability, by extension the term white box testing may sometimes infer a higher level of skill than black box testing. The effect is most often seen in a human resources scenario. A job description may specify that the position requires white box testing. This is sometimes interpreted as meaning the position requires a test engineer who has relatively strong coding ability.

Review Question

Which of the following statements regarding black box and white box testing is true?

a. In general, only black box approaches are necessary when testing most software systems.

b. In general, white box testing would be used in situations where testers are not permitted to view the source code of the system under test because of legal restrictions.

c. In general, use of the term white box or black box may be somewhat useful on a software testing job description to help a human resources department categorize the extent to which the job position requires coding skills.

d. All of the above.

e. None of the above.

4.2 Manual and Automated Testing

Fully automated testing results from test harness programs which launch automatically, execute one or more test cases, log pass / fail results, and record those results in a data store of some kind. Completely manual tests are performed strictly by hand. Many tests are a combination of automated and manual. For example, suppose you are testing a SQL stored procedure named usp_getBookData which accepts a book title and which returns a SQL record-set of information about books which partially match the input title. If you test the stored procedure by typing:

```
exec usp_getBookData("software")
```

into some text based SQL client program and then visually examine the results displayed to determine if the result is correct or not, then you might be classified as performing either manual testing or automated testing, or a combination of the two.

Compared to manual testing, test automation has five advantages that are summarized by the acronym SAPES: speed, accuracy, precision, efficiency, and skill-building. Automated tests can be executed much faster than manual tests. Automated testing is not subject to human error such as incorrectly recording a test result. Automated tests are precise because they normally execute the same way each time they are performed. Automated testing is efficient because the testing can run unattended, freeing a tester for other activities. And the creation of automated tests can often enhance an engineer's personal skill set.

However, automated testing can be expensive to create because writing custom test automation requires testers with significant coding skills. Each development and tester scenario should be evaluated to determine if the time, effort, and expense required to create automated tests are likely to generate a good return on investment value. Automated testing is often very well suited for module testing. Automated UI testing for user application software is often best suited for relatively simple test scenarios.

An alternative to writing custom test automation is to use a commercial test framework or an open source test framework. Compared to writing custom test automation, commercial test frameworks have the disadvantages of high initial cost, a steep learning curve especially when they use a proprietary scripting language, and expensive training costs. Open source test frameworks do not have high initial cost, but they can have unstable code bases, generally have highly variable quality, and may have hidden legal issues. Compared to writing custom test automation, the use of a framework can have the subtle effect of driving a test effort towards the type of testing best suited by the framework rather than the testing required by the system under development. For example, if you are using a tool that has a great record-playback feature, you may easily find yourself performing a lot of record-playback testing instead of creatively designing test scenarios.

The terms verification and validation are often used interchangeably in both manual testing and test automation situations, however technically they have different meanings. Verification is the process of determining whether or not a software system performs according to its functional specifications. Validation is the process of determining whether or not a software system meets its requirements specifications.

Review Question

Which of the following statements best characterizes manual testing and automated testing?

a. Automated testing is generally best used for relatively simple test cases, freeing a tester's time for performing complex test cases.

b. Automated testing in general tends to be more precise than manual testing.

c. Automated test creation in general tends to enhance a tester's skill set more than performing manual testing.

d. All of the above.

e. None of the above.

4.3 Stress and Load Testing

Stress testing is the process of determining if a software system under test meets its functional requirements when operating under conditions of low resources, typically low CPU availability, low

RAM, or limited hard drive space. For example, a functional specification for a system may state something like "the system must be able to respond to a Refresh request within 4000 milliseconds when the processor usage is operating at 95% or less." To verify this requirement is met, a software test engineer would likely use a stress tool that simulates other programs running on a test host machine to throttle up the CPU usage on the test host machine to the desired level and then perform a Refresh operation and measure the response time. There are many tools available to adjust CPU usage, RAM, and available hard drive space.

In practice it is not unusual for the exact behavior of a system running under reduced resources to not be precisely defined in the system's specification document. In this situation stress testing can take the form of starting the system under test with normal usage conditions and then gradually lowering system resources until the system fails. The idea is to determine if the system fails gracefully (for example by saving its current state to disk and then exiting) or if the system simply crashes.

Load testing is closely related to stress testing and the two terms are sometimes used interchangeably. Load testing generally refers to the process of determining if the system under test meets its functional requirements when operating with a large number of users. For example, in the case of a Web application, load testing often takes the form of exercising the Web application when a large number of users are simultaneously connected to the Web site hosting the application. This is normally accomplished through the use of a tool which can simulate many users by programmatically sending HTTP requests to the Web site hosting the Web application. There are many such load tools available, including open source tools, commercial tools, and load tools which are integrated into IDEs such as Visual Studio. Web application load tools are creating stress on the hosting Web server rather than directly on the Web application itself. The term load testing can also apply to situations where the multiple users exercising the system are system processes rather than human users.

Stability testing is another variation of the stress and load testing theme. In stability testing, the system under test is exercised under normal conditions over a long period of time. This is usually done to determine if the SUT has some sort of undetected memory leak. Over time, each operation that causes a memory leak will slowly reduce the amount of available memory until the SUT finally fails. Stability is usually measured as Mean Time To Failure (MTTF) or as Mean Time Between Failures (MTBF). The MTTF is computed by repeatedly starting the SUT and exercising it until it fails. Each elapsed run time is recorded and the MTTF is the arithmetic mean of the elapsed times. The MTBF is very similar except that here the assumption is the SUT is run continuously and the time of each failure (presumably non fatal errors) is recorded. At some point the SUT is stopped and the MTBF is the arithmetic mean of the recorded times.

Review Question

Which of the following scenarios best illustrates stress testing?

a. Testing a software system by sending it invalid input (such as null values, empty strings, zero values, and so on).

b. Testing a software system by using different types of peripheral hardware equipment (such as keyboards, monitors, mice, and so on) on the test host machine.

c. Testing a software system using normal functionality test cases, while the system is operating under a condition of reduced CPU availability due to a processor-intensive dummy application running on the test host machine.

d. Testing a software system by sending the system a set of 100 random inputs.

4.4 Configuration Testing

Configuration testing is the process of testing a system under development on machines which have various combinations of hardware and software. In many situations the number of possible configurations is far too large to test. For example, suppose you are a member of a test team which working on some desktop user application. The number of combinations of operating system versions, memory sizes, hard drive types, CPUs alone could be enormous. If you target only 10 different operating system versions, 8 different memory sizes, 6 different hard drives, and 7 different CPUs, there are already $10 * 8 * 6 * 7 = 3,360$ different hardware configurations. Then if you add various software components such as Web browser version, anti-virus software, earlier versions of the system under development, the number of possible configurations quickly becomes unmanageable. Note that not all software development efforts necessarily face an unmanageable number of configurations. For example, software developed for specific, non-PC hardware devices may have only a handful of hardware and software configurations.

Because the number of possible configurations to test is typically too large to effectively test, it is crucial that the planning effort for a software testing effort clearly identify which platforms will be supported. If, as is often the case, the number of combinations of hardware and software is simply too great to test thoroughly, then the test planning effort must carefully prioritize testing different configurations based on a number of factors such as the size of the user base, and the risk associated with an undiscovered bug in a particular configuration.

Hardware configuration testing is often performed in test labs which simply consist of a large number of machines with different types of hardware. When a testable build of the system under development is released, the build is installed onto each machine in the lab, and a suite of tests is run on each machine. Because there are usually a large number of machines in a test lab, in most situations a significant amount of automation is performed to install the system under test and execute test suites. Setting up a test lab can be expensive so in many situations hardware configuration testing is well suited to outsourcing to organizations which specialize in this type of testing.

Software configuration testing can be very time consuming because of the time required to install and uninstall software including operating system software. For this reason, software configuration testing is also often heavily automated. One configuration testing approach which is not generally possible for hardware testing, but is possible for software testing, is to test on virtual machines. A virtual machine consists of a single file, often called a VHD, or virtual hard drive, which when installed on a host machine can simulate a particular real software configuration. Multiple virtual machines, each with a different software configuration, can be installed and run on a single physical host machine, and tested simultaneously. A software configuration test effort can maintain a library of virtual machines in the form of a set of .vhd files which can be used as needed for testing. There are both commercial virtual machine systems as well as systems which are freely available. On Microsoft platforms, free virtual systems include Virtual PC and the very closely related Virtual Server (the differences between the two are very small and mostly technical in nature), and the 64-bit machine based Hyper-V system. There are several free or open source virtual machine software systems for Unix platforms. One such system is VirtualBox.

Review Question

Which of the following statements best characterizes configuration testing for application software such as a word processor program, a media program, and so on?

a. In most cases application software will run on any reasonable configuration of hardware and software; therefore configuration testing should not be part of the testing effort.

b. In most cases it is quite difficult and costly to perform configuration testing of application software; therefore configuration testing is best performed after the product has been released.

c. In most cases the number of different configurations is under 12; therefore all configurations should be tested before the product is released.

d. In most cases the number of different configurations is far too large to thoroughly test; therefore the test plan should prioritize which configurations will be tested, and which configurations will not be tested.

4.5 Localization Testing

In casual usage, the terms internationalization, localization, and globalization are used somewhat interchangeably to refer to the process of converting a software system from English into some other language. However engineers and managers who work in this area make distinctions between these terms that software test engineers should be aware of. Before defining these three terms it is necessary to understand the concept of a locale. A locale consists of a language (such as English), a country (such as UK), and a set of settings for things like date format (such 01/17/2009) and time format (such as 13:45:00). The language and country combination of locales have specific numeric and text IDs. For example, U.S. English has numeric ID 1033 and text ID en-US. United Kingdom English has numeric ID 2057 and text ID en-UK. Canada French has numeric ID 3084 and text ID fr-CA. Localization is the actual process of transforming a software system from the language in which it was written, such as U.S. English, into some other language such as Germany German.

Internationalization is the process of preparing the source language system for translation. One common approach to internationalization is to design the system in such a way that all parts of the target system which will need to be translated are modularized into so-called resource files. For example, instead of hard-coding a user prompt directly into the system's source code along the lines of:

```
textBox1.Text = "Enter your last name";
```

the developer places all strings into a separate file called a resource file, say en-US.dll for example So the text "Enter your last name" might be assigned to a variable named String1 located inside a resource file which can be programmatically accessed as object Resource1. Then the system code would resemble:

```
textBox1.Text = Resource1.String1;
```

Localization engineers can then translate all the strings used in the system to a different language and then produce a new resource file such as fr-CA.dll. A simple modification of the system source code, or of the build process can indicate that a new build should use the resource DLL file and the result is a version of the system in a different language. Localization can be very tricky. For example, consider the situation where a phrase in English has three words and a total of 15 characters, but the corresponding phrase in German has 42 characters. There could be UI layout issues where the German text won't fit in the space allotted for the English text.

To reiterate, loosely stated, internationalization is the process of preparing a software system for conversion from English to some other language, and localization is the actual process of conversion. The third language-related term is globalization. Globalization is usually used to mean the combined process of internationalization and localization. Less often the term globalization is used to mean the process of converting a software system from English to some other language in such a way that the resulting translation is not offensive. For example, an icon which displays a hand gesture with the thumb sticking up combined with the text "OK" might be fine in English, but the gesture is considered obscene some countries.

Review Question

Which of the following statements best describes the difference between internationalization and localization?

a. The RFC 4646 Standard states that the terms internationalization and localization have identical meaning.

b. Internationalization is the process of translating a software system into a language which uses the Unicode character set; localization is the process of translating a software system into a language which uses the ASCII character set.

c. Internationalization is the process of translating a software system into a language which uses any non-Western alphabet (such as Chinese, Japanese, and Arabic); localization is the process of translating a software system into a language which any Western alphabet (such as English, Spanish, and French).

d. Internationalization is the process of designing a software system so that it can be easily translated into multiple languages; localization is the actual process of translating a software system into a particular language and culture (such as Canada French or Belgium French).

4.6 Record-Playback Testing

Record-playback UI testing is the process of using a software tool which captures a manual user's manipulation of some software application under test. The capture is generally in the form of some type of scripting language. The script which represents the capture can then be executed as is, replicating the manual user's actions, or the script can be edited and then run to produce a new set of actions. Although there are a wide range of opinions on the usefulness of record-playback testing, survey results suggest that the majority of experienced software test engineers believe that record-playback testing has quite limited value when the costs of creating record-playback tests are compared with the number of bugs revealed by these tests.

The primary advantage of using a commercial record-playback tool for UI testing compared to writing custom UI test automation is simplicity. Learning to use a record-playback tool is generally quite easy even for inexperienced testers. However, commercial record-playback tools have several disadvantages. Commercial record-playback tools are generally quite expensive to purchase. Many record-playback tools capture user actions in the form of a custom scripting language. If the record-playback tool is intended for use as a starting point for custom UI test automation, then there can be a significant cost associated with learning the tool's custom scripting language. If a record-playback tool is used only to capture and then rerun a user's manual activity on a software application under test, then testing activities are generally limited to regression testing, that is simply verifying that a new build of the application under test operates in the same way as a previous build of the application. Another disadvantage of using a record-playback tool is that in many cases, a very small change in the application under test will invalidate a captured script, which means that a new script must be captured. A closely related problem is that record-playback tools are generally not well-suited for determining details about the application under test's final state.

There are a number of open source record-playback tools available which address the initial cost objection to commercial tools, however open source tools typically have hidden costs in the form of support, stability, and potential legal problems.

A subtle disadvantage of record-playback tools is a non-technical issue. Survey data suggests that record-playback tools generally do not reveal many bugs in application software compared to alternative testing techniques. However, the execution of record-playback scripts is often impressive to naive observers (such as non-technical management) in part because the visual nature of the playback implies that sophisticated testing actions are occurring behind the scenes when in fact they may not be. This can lead to an over reliance on record-playback testing at the expense of the use of other testing techniques. Overall, the general consensus in survey data from experienced software test engineers is that record-playback testing is most useful for relatively simple regression testing, but is not particularly useful for more complex UI testing.

The main alternative to using a record-playback tool for UI test automation is to write custom automation code. Writing custom UI test automation from scratch using a general purpose programming language such as Java, C++ or C# generally requires highly skilled software test engineers. When written properly, custom test automation can be more flexible and useful than the automation produced by record-playback tools. There are several UI test automation frameworks which are available for writing custom UI test automation. These frameworks provide software test engineers with a library of prewritten code which can speed up the process of writing test automation. Examples include the open source WATIR (Web Application Testing in Ruby) library for automating Web applications which are hosted by the Internet Explorer browser, using the Ruby scripting language, and the MUIA (Microsoft UI Automation) library for automating non-Web applications, using the C# programming language.

Review Question

Which of the following statements about the record-playback approach to software application UI testing best agrees with survey data from experienced software test engineers?

a. In general, record-playback UI testing has virtually no use whatsoever in a software testing effort.

b. In general, record-playback UI testing provides little value to a testing effort except for relatively simple regression testing scenarios.

c. In general, record-playback UI testing is usually considered to be one of the most valuable testing techniques available for application testing but is only moderately valuable for system module testing.

d. In general, record-playback UI testing is usually considered to be one of the most valuable testing techniques available for both system module testing and application testing.

4.7 Random Input Testing

Random input testing is the process of sending random input to the system under test. In most situations, because the input is random, there is no way to determine an expected result. Therefore, the goal of random input testing is often to cause a system crash or hang. Additionally, when no explicit test cases are used, random input testing is generally simple and quick to implement in many test efforts. Random input testing is usually automated but can be performed manually as well. Random input testing is sometimes called fuzz testing or robustness testing.

There are many variations of random input testing. The system under test can be reset to an initial state before each random input is submitted, or the SUT can be allowed to transition from state to state for each random input. Input can be completely random, and the input can be constrained in some way to generate input within certain limits. For example, consider a Web application which has an input text box with maxlength attribute set to 5 characters for a user to enter a postal zip code. Random input testing can be designed to send any five characters which can be generated by keyboard input (such as "1Q;w7") to the input field, or any five characters in hexadecimal form, even those characters which cannot be directly generated by the keyboard, or just any five digit characters, or any number of digit characters, and so on. In the case of manual random input testing, software testers often use a utility program to generate a list of random input and then manually enter the input into the SUT. In the case of automated random input testing, the test harness often does not read a test case data file. More often, the logic of the types of random input to produce is coded directly into the test harness. Alternatively, test case data for random input testing can be created which contains input constraints. For example:

```
S001 : 1000000 : 5 : A : Z
S002 : 500000 : x : 0 : 9
etc.
```

Here, the first line could be interpreted by the test harness as meaning, "For random input scenario #001, generate 1,000,000 random inputs, all of length 5 characters, where each character is in the range upper case A through upper case Z." Then the second line could mean, "For random input scenario #002, generate 500,000 random inputs, with a random length, where each character is in the range digit 0 through digit 9.

In the previous comments the term random inputs is used. True random input is difficult to create and is not reproducible. Therefore in almost all random input testing scenarios pseudorandom numbers are used. Most programming languages have a library function which generates pseudorandom numbers. For example, in the C# programming language, the statements:

```
Math.Random r = new Math.Random(99);
int roll = r.Next(0,7);
```

can be used to simulate the roll of one of a pair of dice. The first statement initializes a Random object with a seed value of 99. The seed value is arbitrary and indirectly sets the internal starting point for the pseudo random number generator. If no seed value is supplied to the Random object constructor, a seed value based on the current date and time is generated and used. The second line generates a random integer which is greater than or equal to 0 and strictly less than 7, or symbolically, variable roll is in the range [0,7) (or more readably, [0,6]). In random input testing, a seed value is usually supplied to the constructor method so that the test run can be replicated if necessary.

Review Question

Which of the following statements is most often true about random input testing?

a. In most situations with random input testing, the test case expected result is null (if the expected item is an object), or 0 (if the expected item is numeric), or the empty string (if the expected item is a string).

b. In most situations with random input testing, the pseudorandom number generator function which is used, is initialized with a random seed value determined by the system date and time on the test host machine.

c. In most situations with random input testing, it is not possible to have an explicit expected result, so the implicit expected result is a system crash, hang, or exception of some sort.

d. All of the above.

e. None of the above.

CHAPTER 5
ESSENTIAL KNOWLEDGE

Many software testing books do a good job of describing core software testing principles and defining vocabulary. And there are many books and online resources which explain specific testing techniques. The seven topics in this chapter fall between those two extremes in the sense that they provide more guidance for performing testing activities than definitions but fall short of describing step-by-step testing procedures.

5.1 Character Encoding

Most software systems deal with text data. The most fundamental form of text data is the character data type. The simplest form of character data encoding is the ASCII (American Standard Code for Information Interchange) character set. With ASCII, each character is encoded using 7 bits, which gives a total of 128 possible characters. Because most computers work with bytes of size 8 bits, extended ASCII uses the extra bit for a total of 256 possible characters. For example, character 'A' (upper case A) is encoded as:

```
0100-0001
```

which is also 65d (decimal) or 41h (hexadecimal). ASCII was invented in the 1960s and is still in common use. With the creation of the Internet in the 1990s and the need for non-English language support, the Unicode character scheme was invented. Each character has a Unicode number but can be encoded in three main ways: UTF-8, UTF-16, and UTF-32.

The UTF-32 (Unicode Transformation Format, 32-bits) version of Unicode uses exactly 32 bits for each character. So, there are a total of 2^{32} = 4,294,967,296 possible UTF-32 encodings (but not all are used). The UTF-32 encoding for 'A' is:

```
0000-0000 0000-0000 0000-0000 0100-0001
```

which uses up four times as much memory as ASCII. UTF-32 is efficient for use with internal data on machines which have a lot of memory, but is not very efficient for data which is transmitted and received across a network. The UTF-8 and UTF-16 versions of Unicode are variable length, meaning that different characters have different sizes. The details of UTF-8 and UTF-16 are a bit complicated. UTF-8 stores characters using 8 bits, 16 bits, 24 bits, or 32 bits, depending on the character. For simple characters in the range 0-255d, ASCII and UTF-8 encodings are the same so ASCII and UTF-8 are somewhat compatible. For characters beyond the range of 255d, the first few bits of UTF-8 encoding indicate how many bits are being used to store the character and the remaining bits represent the character. For example, the Hebrew character "alef" is Unicode character number 05D0h. It is encoded in UTF-8 with 16 bytes as:

```
1101-0111 1001-0000
```

The three leading 110 bits indicate that the character is encoded using 16 bits. UTF-16 encoding stores each character using either 16 bits or 32 bits. Conversion between different character encodings can be very tricky. ASCII is often used for simple text files. UTF-8 is often used for XML files because such files are often sent over networks. UTF-16 is the native string type for Windows operating systems, the .NET Framework, and the Java programming language. UTF-32 is used internally on some Unix-based operating systems.

Review Question

Which of the following is the correct UTF-8 Unicode encoding for character 'z' (lower case letter z which has ASCII value 122d = 7Ah = 01111010b)?

a. 0111 1010

b. 0000 0111 1010

c. 0000 0000 0111 1010

d. 1111 1111 0111 1010

5.2 XML and Testing

XML (Extensible Markup Language) is a specification for describing data. In software testing, XML is used for many purposes including storing test case data, test result data, test harness configuration data, and so on. Although XML is simple in principle, working with XML files can be somewhat tricky in certain scenarios. An important distinction is the difference between well-formed XML and valid XML. Well-formed XML meets all the general syntax requirements of the W3C (World Wide Web Consortium) XML specification, such as each XML begin-element tag must have a corresponding end-element. On the other hand, valid XML meets a set of specific system-defined rules such as, "All <author> elements must contain at least one <lastName> element." The two most common ways to specify a set of system-defined rules are to use a DTD (Document Type Definition) file, or use an XSD (XML Schema Definition) file. DTD is an older text based scheme and XSD is a newer XML based scheme.

Another distinction is the difference between an XML document and an XML fragment. An XML document has a beginning declaration and a root element such as:

```
<?xml version="1.0" encoding="UTF-8" ?>
<authors>
  . . .
</authors>
```

An XML fragment is part of an XML document, typically an element (which may have sub-elements).

Information in XML is normally stored in one of two main ways: in an element, or as an attribute. For example:

```
<testCase id="001">
 <input1>5</input1>
 <input2>3</input2>
 <expected>8</expected>
</testCase>
```

In this example, id is an attribute with value 001, and input1 is an element with value 5. There are several technologies which are closely related to XML including:

XSLT (Extensible Stylesheet Language Transformations) is a declarative language specification typically used to create a template which in turn is used to transform an XML document into a second XML document with a different structure.

XQuery is a language used to both extract information from an XML document and to transform an XML document.

XPath is a language used to extract information from an XML document.

XSL-FO (Extensible Stylesheet Language Formatting Objects) is a language used to format the display of XML data.

Review Question

Which of the following technologies is commonly used to transform XML from one format to another?

a. XSD (XML Schema Definition).

b. DTD (Document Type Definition).

c. XSLT (Extensible Stylesheet Language Transformations).

d. XQuery.

e. Both a. and b.

f. Both c. and d.

g. None of the above.

5.3 HTTP Request-Response Testing

HTTP request-response testing is arguably the most fundamental type of testing for Web applications. Consider a Web application under test which has a Form in the client area defined by:

```
<form action='makePage.asp' method='get'>
 <input type='text' name='title' value='Enter ti-
tle'/>
  <input  type='text'  name='price'  value='Enter
price'/>
 <input type='submit' />
</form>
```

The Web application would display a text box containing the text "Enter title", a second text box containing the text "Enter price", and a button control with a default label of "Submit Query". Notice the action and method attributes of the Form element. If a user types in some text into the two text box controls and then clicks the submit button, the values in the two text box controls will be sent to the Web server using the GET method, along with a request to execute a script named makePage.asp which presumably creates a Web page, using the title and price values in some way, in the form of an HTML stream. The newly created Web page is sent back to the user as a response where the user's Web browser will display the newly created page in human-friendly form.

Most Web applications use either the GET method, as in the example above, or the POST method. When a Web application specifies method='get', the values contained in the Form element are sent as ordinary text appended to the action URL as name-value pairs separated by the '&' character. Blank spaces are encoded as a '+' character. This called a query string. So, suppose the Web application above is located at http://localhost/TheWebApp.html and a user types 'test it' into the title box and '12.34' into the price box, and then clicks on the submit button, the Form information is sent to the Web server as:

```
http://localhost/makePage.asp?title=test+it&price=
12.34
```

This mechanism allows a test engineer to perform manual or automated HTTP request-response testing in a relatively simple way. For example, a tester can directly enter information such as the example above into the address bar of a Web browser and then examine the result page to determine a pass/fail result. The technique can also be made more efficient using automation by writing a simple test harness which programmatically sends a sequence of query string input requests to the Web server, fetches the resulting HTML response, and examines that response programmatically for an expected value of some sort. Most programming languages have a library module of some sort which makes sending an HTTP request relatively easy.

In the example above, the Form action is to execute a script named makePage.asp. ASP is a technology which uses the VBScript language by default. The same HTTP request-response principles apply to CGI technology (which uses Perl), ASP.NET technology (which uses C# or VB.NET), JSP technology (which uses Java), and PHP technology (which uses the PHP language).

Web applications can also use the POST method to send Form information to a Web server. The POST mechanism does not send Form information as a query string appended to a URL. POST data is embedded into the body of the associated HTTP request. This means a manual approach such as described above is not possible, but an automated approach which programmatically embeds test case input data into an HTTP request is feasible.

Review Question

Suppose you are manually testing a Web application that accepts user input from an HTML Form element and uses the GET method along the lines of:

```
<form action='buildPage.asp' method='get'>
 <input type='text' name='city' />
 <input type='text' name='state' />
 <input type='submit' />
</form>
```

Which of the following represents a valid test case input when typed into the address bar of a Web browser?

a. http://localhost/buildPage.asp::city=Bay City::state=RI

b. http://localhost/buildPage.asp/city/Bay,City/state/RI

c. http://localhost/buildPage.asp?city=Bay+City&state=RI

d. http://localhost/buildPage.asp\\city,Bay%20City\\state,RI

5.4 HTTP State Testing

In order to effectively test Web applications, software test engineers must have a basic understanding of how Web applications maintain state. HTTP is said to be a stateless protocol because by default every HTTP request sent to a Web server is processed, a resulting HTML stream is created and returned to the client, and then forgotten by the Web server. This mechanism is perfect in situations where a client Web browser simply requests a Web page and just displays the returned page. However, for any situation where sequences of Web pages in a user session are related in some way, a stateless protocol is awkward. For example, imagine a Web application which has a large Form element with many input fields for user information such as First Name, Last Name, Street Address, City, State, Zip Code, and so on. Imagine that after a user fills in all the input fields and clicks on a submit button to send the Form data to the Web server for processing, the processing script determines that there is an error of some sort such as missing Zip Code data. If the processing script sends back an error page, by default, all the information entered by the user will be lost, and the user will have to re-enter all the Form data.

There are several ways that a Web developer can work around the default stateless HTTP request-response mechanism so that a Web application can maintain state. One common approach is for the Web developer to write script code which programmatically inserts a hidden (to the user) field into a Form element on a Web application. For example, an HTML element such as <input type='hidden' name='state' value='NY' /> holds user input. If the Form is submitted with action='post' the hidden data will be placed into the body of the HTTP request and sent to the server. If the Form is submitted with action='get' the hidden data will be sent as a query string. In either case the hidden data can be viewed by the user (by doing a browser view-source or by observing the query string). The hidden input field technique can be considered somewhat of a hybrid client-server technique because state information in some sense exists in the message streams between the client program and the Web server. Some disadvantages of using the hidden input field technique compared to other approaches are that the technique can be somewhat difficult for developers to code, and if the number of hidden input fields is very large, there may be a performance effect because all hidden data is passed back and forth from client to server on each HTTP request-response operation. Information is hidden fields is only available during a particular HTTP user session and is lost when the client disconnects from a Web site.

An alternative client-side technique to maintain Web application state is the use of HTTP Cookies. Cookies are small text files that are passed back and forth between client browser and Web server much like hidden input fields. However, Cookies have an expiration date/time. If the expiration time is immediate then the Cookie file vanishes when the user's client-server session ends. But if the expiration date is set to some date/time in the future, when the client-server session ends the Cookie is saved on the client machine's hard drive. Therefore the data in Cookies can persist even after the user disconnects from a Web site. Cookies contain the name of the Web site to which they belong, so every time a client Web browser sends an HTTP request to a Web server that has an associated Cookie, the information in the Cookie is sent to the server. The Web server can then read the data and use it to construct a new Web page. One disadvantage of the use of Cookies to maintain Web state is that users can select to disable cookies.

A third technique for maintaining HTTP state is the use of Web server session and application objects. Most Web server software such as IIS (Internet Information Services) and Apache provide some form of built-in mechanism to store session or application data on the server. Application data is stored and available for all users who are currently accessing a particular Web application. Session data is stored and available only to a particular user/session. The primary disadvantage of using session or application objects on the server is that if there are a large number of users connected, the storage requirements can be very large, which in turn can slow server performance even when the session and application data is stored on separate SQL database server machines.

Review Question

Suppose you are testing a Web application. Two different client machines, both using the same operating system and Web browser, are responding slightly differently to the Web application so you suspect there may an HTTP state issue of some sort. Which of the following is most likely the best place to begin checking your hunch?

a. Examine the Cookies on the two client machines' hard drives to see if there are any differences.

b. Examine the single Application State object on the Web Server.

c. Check the network connections settings on the two Web browsers.

d. Check the security settings on the network domain controller.

5.5 Testing Database-Centric Applications

Some of the most common types of software applications are database-centric programs. Examples include an online bookstore Web application and a desktop auto parts inventory system. Database-centric systems usually consist of a front end user interface (typically a Web page or a desktop Form application), a back end SQL database, and a logical middle tier which contains various business rules. Database-centric programs are often said to perform CRUD operations on their underlying database: create, read, update, and delete. Testing database-centric applications poses special problems. In some situations, software development engineers design and code all three components (front end, back end, middle tier). In some situations each of these three tasks is performed by separate engineers or teams of engineers. In any case, during the development process software front end and middle tier design engineers generally have their own private copies of the back end database. This copy is sometimes called a database testbed (or test bed). The term testbed can have many different meanings in other contexts. This database copy is used for the normal ad hoc testing which occurs during the development process. It is generally not feasible for developers to use the actual production database for development activities.

Similarly, it is generally not possible for software test engineers to thoroughly test a database-centric application using the production database because thorough testing will involve all types of activities which may corrupt or permanently delete data in the database. Additionally, it is generally not advisable to simply use the developer database testbed for testing because data which is typically housed in a testbed used for development purposes is often not rich enough in variety for testing purposes. For example, a database testbed for testing purposes will likely contain data not found in a developer testbed or production database, such as many SQL null values, and illegal values.

In short, when developing a database-centric software application it is not uncommon for there to be several different versions of the production database, where each version has the identical structure (tables, stored procedures, relationships, users, and so on) but different data. Therefore it is important for a testing effort to be synchronized with the efforts that are creating the backend database. A common way to manage this synchronization issue is to use a source/version control tool to manage database creation scripts. In this way, any member of the overall development effort can easily create the structure of the current version of the system's back end database simply by executing the current SQL script.

In many situations the front end of the application under development interacts with the back end database through the use of SQL stored procedures or by using C#, Java, C++ or similar code in the middle tier, or by some combination of these two approaches. So one approach to testing database-centric applications is to create a database testbed, populate the testbed with interesting data, and then perform module testing through one of the interfaces to the database. Although creating a SQL database structure is generally not too difficult if a software test engineer has a SQL creation script, populating the database with data can be very time consuming. Furthermore, it can sometimes be challenging to verify the state of a database after some test case input has modified the database. In many situations it is not feasible to check every aspect of a database after some operation. For example, suppose you are testing an application that manages book store inventory where book data is contained in three different SQL tables. If some test case deletes book information from the database, you would certainly check to verify that the appropriate rows in the three tables were correctly deleted but it may not be practical to examine every row in every table to verify that no other rows were accidentally deleted.

Review Question

Suppose you are testing a Web based, database-centric software application which is under development and has not yet been released to the public. Which of the following statements is most likely to be true?

a. In order to test the application you will likely need to create a testbed database which is different from the development database and different from the production database.

b. In order to test the application you will likely need to use only the development database.

c. In order to test the application you will likely need to use only the production database.

d. In order to test the application you will likely not need to use any database.

5.6 Copying Files

One of the most fundamental tasks test engineers perform when working in a software development environment is copying files from one machine to another. Most Windows based networks are conceptually organized around a user's local machine which has a relatively large hard disk drive which contains the user's home root directory, typically labeled as the C: drive. Most Unix based networks are conceptually organized as a set of distributed files across multiple machines where a user's host machine acts primarily as a portal to a file system. A Unix user's home directory is often located on a remote file server rather than the user's local machine, and is often accessed through the '~' alias.

In a Windows environment, copying a file or set of files from a remote machine to a local machine is typically performed using the xcopy command in conjunction with a network shared directory, or network share for short. For example, a user who holds administrative privileges on a machine can designate a directory as shared which allows other users on the network to view and copy files from the share. Permissions can also be set on a shared directory which allows users to copy files into the share. A user on a local machine can copy files from a remote machine to local machine along the lines of:

```
C:\Here> xcopy \\otherMachineName\shareName\file-
Name.txt C:\Here\Foo\
```

This command copies file 'fileName.txt' from the shared directory named shareName which is located on a remote machine named otherMachineName, to a directory C:\Here\Foo on the local machine. When using the xcopy command, the remote machine can also be identified using the machine's IP address such as \\192.168.0.43\shareName\fileName.txt. When copying files using xcopy, a trailing '\' on the destination argument is sometimes important to indicate that the target is a directory rather than a new file name to be assigned to the copied file. In other words, the same command above without a trailing '\' could be interpreted to mean copy file fileName.txt to local directory C:\Here and then rename the copied file as Here (without any extension).

In order to copy a single file, software test engineers can use the Windows Explorer GUI tool. However, when copying multiple files, or when copying files programmatically using .bat script files, using the xcopy command is often a more efficient technique.

An alternative to using explicitly named remote machines and shared network directories in a Windows environment is to use the shared drive mechanism which essentially creates an alias for a remote machine and network share. For example the command:

```
C:\Here> net use x: \\otherMachineName\shareName
```

creates a virtual drive named X: which references the remote share. The alias can be used just as the fully qualified path could be used:

```
C:\Here> cd X:
X:\> xcopy fileName.txt C:\Here\Foo\
X:\> cd C:\Here
C:\Here> net use x: /delete
```

The net use command with a /delete argument deletes the network share alias name, not the network share.

In a Unix environment, copying files from a remote machine to a local machine happens less often than in a Windows environment because many Unix file systems are distributed and so files are normally copied from directory to directory transparently using the cp (copy) command. However, in situations where an explicit file copy from remote to local machine is necessary, there are several Unix programs which can be used. One such program is rcp (remote copy) which is an older program that copies files without using any form of encryption. The rcp command typically relies on a file called .rhosts (remote hosts) to determine if the copy operation is authorized or not. When a secure file copy mechanism is needed, many Unix systems have a scp (secure copy) program which acts much like rcp except that file transfers are encrypted.

On both Windows and Unix systems, an alternative for copying files from a remote machine to a local machine is some variation of a program usually named FTP (file transfer protocol). For FTP file transfers, the remote machine must be set up to act as an FTP server. A simplified example of FTP usage is:

```
C:\> ftp remoteMachineName
ftp> cd \directoryName
ftp> ls
ftp> bin
ftp> get fileName.txt
ftp> exit
C:\>
```

These commands connect to a remote machine, navigate (cd) to directory directoryName on the remote machine, list (ls) the contents of the remote directory, indicate that file transfers should be performed in raw binary format (bin), and copy (get) file fileName. txt from the remote machine to the local machine.

Review Question

Assuming you have appropriate network permissions, which of the following sets of cmd.exe shell commands will copy all files with a .txt extension from directory C:\Data\Tests on a local machine named Alpha, to a network shared directory named Public located on remote machine named Beta?

```
a. C:\Gamma> net use x: \\Beta\Public
   C:\Gamma> xcopy C:\Data\Tests\*.txt x:
   C:\Gamma> net use /delete x:
b. C:\Gamma> cd C:\\Beta\Public
   C:\Public> copy local\Alpha\*.txt C:\Public
c. C:\Gamma> delete C:\Data\Tests\*.txt
   C:\Gamma> restore *.txt \\Beta\Public\
d. C:\Gamma> copy C:\Data\Tests \\local\clip
   C:\Gamma> copy \\local\clip \\Beta\C$\Public
```

5.7 Network Troubleshooting

Network connectivity problems are common. The essence of successfully troubleshooting most systems with multiple components is to perform different actions which will isolate the problem. Troubleshooting a network connectivity problem illustrates this principle. Suppose you are logged on to some local host machine named Alpha and you wish to copy a file from a public share directory named Public on some remote machine named Beta to your local machine. You launch the GUI Windows Explorer program and type \\Beta\Public into the address bar. After a few seconds you receive a generic error message indicating that the Windows Explorer program cannot find the target remote machine. In addition to the troubleshooting principle of isolating the problem, in most situations you should start by performing actions which are relatively quick and easy, and which reveal common problems. In the case of network connectivity problems, doing something as simple as checking that the local host machine's network cable is attached to the machine's NIC is a reasonable first step to take. Equivalently, you can check the network adapter status to see if the adapter is currently connected. After checking the network cable, you might want to issue an ipconfig.exe command from a command shell on the local machine to see if the machine has a valid IP address for your network.

After checking the physical network connection and using the ipconfig.exe tool, a reasonable next step is to try and access a different remote resource from the local machine. If you succeed in connecting to a machine on the network, then you have some measure of confidence that the problem is not with the local machine itself and that the problem is either the remote machine or some component between the local and remote machines such as the domain controller. Similarly, you might want to try to access the remote machine using a different local machine if one is available nearby.

Another standard technique to isolate network connectivity problems is to use the ping command. First, attempt to ping the target remote machine by name, for example C:\>ping Beta. If pinging by name fails with an error message that the request timed out, then attempt to ping the remote machine by IP address, if the address of the remote machine is known, for example C:\>ping 192.168.0.13. If the ping by name fails but the ping by IP address succeeds then the problem may lie with the DNS service which translates machine IP addresses to machine names. In general, when troubleshooting you should try isolation activities which are more complex and take longer only after trying simpler, quicker approaches. For example, in general rebooting a machine or turning a machine off to examine the hardware components should be done only after the steps described above.

In job interviews, hiring managers will sometimes ask questions that attempt to reveal if the job candidate understands the troubleshooting principles of component isolation and trying simple tasks before harder tasks. For example, one such interview question runs along the lines of, "Suppose you enter a room and turn on the light switch. The light fixture on the ceiling does not turn on. How would you go about troubleshooting this situation?" The hiring manager would expect the candidate to describe the overall system involved (building circuit breakers, the primary power line into the building, light switches, and so on) and explain simple tasks such as verifying that the light fixture has a light bulb, and trying a different switch in the room if one exists.

Review Question

Suppose you are troubleshooting a network connectivity problem from a particular local host machine to a remote machine. After checking the physical cable connections on the local machine, which of the following is most likely the best next action for you to take to determine what the problem is?

a. Perform a Windows Repair of the local host machine using the original operating system installation disk.

b. Attempt to access a different remote machine using the local host machine.

c. Replace the NIC (network interface card) on the local host machine.

d. Reboot the local host machine.

CHAPTER 6
UNITS, MODULES, AND COMPONENTS

Most large software systems handle complexity by hierarchically decomposing the system into units and modules. Many software activities involve these components and so understanding them is important. The topics in this chapter are all related to how software system components are organized and communicate.

6.1 Dynamic Link Libraries

Many Windows based software programs, including the Windows operating system itself, are composed of modules which are loaded into memory at run time as the program needs them. These dynamic modules usually take the form of files with a .dll (dynamic link library) file extension, or less commonly an .ocx or .drv extension. Native Win32 DLLs are normally written using the C++ programming language. Most native Win32 DLLs can be categorized as being either standard or COM-based. Standard Win32 DLLs can be called only by programs which are written in the same language in which the DLLs were written — almost always C++. A COM-based Win32 DLL on the other hand, if the DLL is implemented in a special way called dual interface, can be called by programs written in many different languages including C++, Visual Basic, JavaScript, VBScript, C#, VB.NET and so on. In general, programs which use standard Win32 DLLs and COM-based DLLs not implemented with a dual interface, will look for the DLL being called in the current directory (that is, the same directory as the program executable) or in a location which is specified in some way by the calling program. This mechanism for finding dynamic libraries is non-trivial and is a common source of trouble when performing many types of software testing.

Dynamic Link Libraries which are COM-based and which implement a dual interface must use a different scheme for specifying their location because the different potential calling languages work in different ways. The location information for these types of DLLs is stored in the Windows system registry. The regsvr32.exe program is used to register such DLLs. The system registry contains the filename of the DLL (such as MyLibrary.dll), its location on the host machine (such as C:\Program Files\Qix), a unique identifier called a CLSID (class ID) in the form of a GUID (Globally Unique Identifier) such as 4E3613F1-3A79-01C2-6F0B-3755B83C9103, and a string identifier called a ProgId (programmatic identifier) such as MyMathLib.MyFunctionsClass.

Encountering problems which arise with DLLs is sometimes informally called DLL hell. These problems can take several different forms that affect testing. Here's one somewhat simplified scenario: Application A, which contains some dynamic link library X.dll, is installed onto a test host machine in a central location such as the C:\Windows\system32 directory. Application B, which also contains an X.dll file, but which is slightly different from the X.dll associated with Application A is then installed, overwriting the X.dll from Application A. At this point Application A may not work.

Review Question

Suppose you are testing some application which contains several COM-based, dual interface Win32 DLL modules. You search the system registry by file name for one of the DLLs. Which of the following items of information are you most likely to find associated with the DLL in the registry?

a. An entry specifying the language in which the DLL was written.

b. A list of users who are authorized to modify the DLL.

c. An MD5 crypto-hash of the contents of the DLL.

d. A ProgId for the DLL for use by scripting languages.

6.2 The Global Assembly Cache

One way to think about the .NET environment is to consider it as a virtual extension of the Windows operating system. Windows operating systems beginning with Windows XP contain a large library of code called the .NET Framework. This library can be accessed by application programmers, greatly speeding up the development process. The .NET Framework is organized into collections called namespaces, such as the System.Data.SqlClient namespace which contains useful code for programs which must connect to and access a SQL database. The physical manifestation of a namespace is an assembly realized in a managed DLL such as a System.Data. SqlClient.dll file. The DLL files which make up the .NET Framework are located in various places throughout a host machine's file system. However there is one central data repository on each host machine which holds the information for all the components of the .NET Framework, such as specific file location and version number. This central repository is called the Global Assembly Cache (GAC). The location of the GAC varies depending upon the version of the Windows operating system on the host machine, but is generally located in a directory such as C:\Windows\assembly.

Viewing the information in the GAC can cause confusion for beginners. If a user launches the GUI Windows Explorer program and navigates to the location of the GAC, the view displayed is a virtual view of a summary the GAC contents rather than a normal file system view. However, if a user launches a shell such as cmd.exe or PowerShell and uses the cd command to navigate to the location of the GAC and then uses the dir command to view the contents, a normal file system view is displayed. In many testing scenarios a good way to view the contents of the GAC is to use the gacutil.exe (GAC utility) command line tool with a /l (list) argument.

The GAC is primarily intended to house .NET assemblies which are shared in the sense that they can be used by multiple programs installed on a test host machine. In most situations, .NET application programs which contain custom assemblies store those assemblies into a directory that is specific to the application — that is the assemblies are not shared. This isolation prevents some of the issues with shared components which give rise to a situation called DLL hell. However, a custom assembly may be stored into the GAC in a situation where the assembly is meant to be used by multiple applications. In order to do so, the custom assembly must be strongly named which means the assembly contains a digital ID based on a crypto-hash of the contents which is in turn encrypted using public key encryption. There are several ways to generate a strong name for a custom assembly which is intended to be placed in the GAC. The sn.exe (strong name) command line tool is one such program. After a custom assembly is given a strong name, the assembly can be stored into the GAC using the gacutil.exe tool with a /i (install) argument.

Review Question

Suppose you are testing a .NET based application which uses an assembly located in the Global Assembly Cache (GAC) on a test host machine. Which of the following tools is most likely the best way to view the contents of the GAC?

a. sn.exe

b. viewgac.exe

c. gacutil.exe

d. cmd.exe

e. None of the above tools can be used to view the contents of the GAC.

6.3 Module Testing

Module testing is arguably the most fundamental type of software testing. Most non-trivial software systems are composed of basic building blocks such as DLLs (dynamic link libraries) and .NET assemblies in a Windows environment, SOs (shared object files) in a Unix-like environment, and Java packages. The idea underlying module testing is simple: if the basic building blocks which make up a software system are not correct, then the software system as a whole cannot possibly be correct. In a Windows development environment the most common scenario is that developers create a library composed of one of more classes which in turn contain one or more methods which must be tested. When developers use native Win32 code (typically with the C++ language) the result is a usually file with a .dll extension. Native code often, but not always, uses COM technology so that the module library can be called from multiple languages such as C++, C#, and JavaScript. Testing modules which are part of a custom library or an operating system (such as user32.dll and shell32.dll modules of the Windows operating system) that are exposed for use by applications programs is sometimes called API (application programming interface) testing. When developers use managed .NET code (typically with the

C# or VB.NET language) the result is also usually a file with a .dll extension although the internal structure is entirely different from a native code DLL file. Managed code libraries do not use COM technology — in fact one of the motivations for creating the .NET environment was to reduce the need for programming with the very difficult to use COM.

Here's a simplified example. Suppose a developer is part of a team working on a software system which performs some mathematical calculations including the harmonic mean of two numbers. (The arithmetic mean is a normal average; the harmonic mean is an average used when the data points are rates such as speed measured in miles per hour). The developer uses C++ to create a COM based, dual interface library module named MyMathLib.dll which contains a class named MyMathFunctions which in turn contains a method HarmonicMean (). At this point the developer could check the new C++ source code into a source code repository where it would eventually be compiled, perhaps by a build team, and the HarmonicMean() method would be available for other developers to use in the software system and for testers to test. An alternative approach is for the developer to request a buddy test. Here the developer would not check the library source code into the source code repository. Instead the developer would compile the source and then give the resulting DLL to a test engineer. The test engineer would then test the methods in the DLL. For example, if using JavaScript, the tester could copy the DLL to a test host machine. Then the tester would register the DLL on the test host using the regsvr32.exe tool and create a small JavaScript test harness that tests the method in the DLL along the lines of:

```
WScript.Echo("Begin test\n");
var obj = new
 ActiveXObject("MyMathLib.MyMathFunctions");
var actualResult = obj.HarmonicMean(30,60);
var expectedResult = 40;
if (actualResult == expectedResult)
 WScript.Echo("Pass");
else
 WScript.Echo("Fail");
```

One of the ideas of buddy testing is to have some measure of confidence that new source code is relatively free of bugs before the code is checked into a source code repository.

Review Question

Suppose you are a tester and have been asked to perform a buddy test on a method named Encode() which resides in a class named MyCryptoRoutines which in turn resides in a library module compiled to a MyCryptoLib.dll file. The Encode() method was developed with the C++ language using COM technology with a dual interface. Which of the following programming languages can you use to call and test the Encode() method?

a. The C++ language.

b. The C# language.

c. The JavaScript language.

d. All of the above.

e. None of the above.

6.4 Unit Testing

The term unit testing can have several different meanings. In most situations, unit testing refers to a technique, used by a developer while writing an object oriented library, which tests the methods in the library more or less at the same time as the code is written. This process, where a developer writes and tests code in parallel is often called test driven development. Here's an example. Suppose a developer is creating some library, using a programming language such as C# or Java, which houses a set of classes and methods which model a deck of cards. One such method might model dealing one card from a deck of cards:

```
class Deck {
 private Card[] cards = null;
 . . .
 public Deck() { . . . }
 public Card Deal() { . . . }
 . . .
}
```

In a classic testing situation, the library would be compiled and then tested using a separate test harness and/or manual testing. This traditional testing process is often called module testing to distinguish it from unit testing. Unit testing allows a developer to directly insert test related code into the library along the lines of:

```
[TestFixture]
public class DealTest {
 [Test]
 public void DealCard() { . . . }
 . . .
}
```

Then, when the library with unit test code is compiled, the library now contains an executable DealCard() test which can be quickly run from a GUI utility program. There is a family of unit test frameworks available. For example, JUnit can be used for unit testing with Java libraries, and NUnit can be used with C# libraries. Additionally, many developer IDE tools contain integrated unit testing functionality.

In general, unit testing is a developer activity and does not thoroughly test the system under development. Unit testing is usually considered a development paradigm and does not eliminate the need for additional, thorough traditional testing. Unit testing complements and supplements traditional testing paradigms and techniques; unit testing is not intended to replace traditional techniques.

Review Question

Which of the following statements best characterizes unit testing with one of the xUnit family of test frameworks such as NUnit or JUnit?

a. Unit testing is primarily a tester activity and is typically used to test methods of the system under test after each stable release of the system.

b. Unit testing is primarily a program manager activity and is typically used for integration testing between the system under test and other existing systems.

c. Unit testing is primarily a developer activity and is typically used to test methods of the system under test during system development.

d. Unit testing is primarily a database developer activity and is typically used to test methods of the system under test which access one or more backend databases associated with the system.

6.5 Kernel Debugging

Most operating systems, including Windows and Unix variants, are designed in multiple layers. The lowest layer is called the kernel. Kernel code interacts directly with the hardware components of a machine, including system memory (RAM), the CPU, and IO devices such as the keyboard, mouse, display monitors and so on. Therefore, software which is not part of the operating system, but which must interact with hardware devices has to have access to the operating system kernel. Such software programs are called device drivers. For example, suppose you create some new type of external storage hardware. You must write device driver software that allows your external storage hardware to communicate with the operating system running on the machine to which the device is attached. This situation is in contrast to most software application programs. Applications typically do not interact directly with hardware devices; applications usually interact with hardware indirectly by calling functions in the operating system designed to do this. These functions are often called API (Application Programming Interface) sets. Application programs are said to run in user mode rather than kernel mode.

The distinction between user mode software and kernel mode software is relevant to testing. In most cases when application software contains a crashing bug, the application itself may crash but the operating system will usually keep running. However when kernel mode software, often device drivers, crashes the entire operating system may be brought down. In a Windows environment this is sometimes called the blue screen of death (BSOD) because of the color of the error screen displayed after a system crash. Ordinary debugging is the process of determining the cause of a software application failure. Ordinary debugging can be accomplished in several ways because after a crash the host machine is still operating and the crashed program can be examined. For example in a Windows environment, testers can use the cdb.exe (command line debugger) or use the integrated debugging capabilities of the Visual Studio integrated development environment. Kernel debugging is the process of determining the cause of an operating system crash. Kernel debugging requires special tools because after a system crash there is no way to directly examine the host machine.

In a Windows environment, a common kernel debugging tool is the kdb.exe (kernel debugger) command line program. Unix variants usually have similar programs, for example, kdbg for use with the Linux kernel. The kdb.exe tool is somewhat tricky to use and so in Windows environment most kernel debugging is performed using the windbg.exe tool which provides a GUI interface around both cdb.exe (for application debugging) and kdb.exe (for kernel debugging). There are two ways to capture an image of a crashed test host machine for analysis by the windbg.exe / kdb.exe tool. First, a tester can configure the test host to save an image of itself after a system crash, typically as a file named MEMORY.DMP directly on the host. Then after a crash, the test host machine is restarted and the memory image can be analyzed using the kdb.exe tool. The second alternative is to connect the test host machine to a second machine, using an RS-232 interface with a null modem cable. Then when the test host crashes, its memory image is sent to the second machine where it can be analyzed.

In a Windows environment, to perform kernel debugging a tester must have a .pdb file (program database) which is specific to the operating system running on the test host machine. The .pdb file can be downloaded from a publicly available database of such files maintained by Microsoft, or in the situation where the test host machine is connected to a second analysis machine; the analysis machine can access the library of .pdb files over the Internet via a Web server maintained by Microsoft. In some situations software testers are responsible for generating and capturing system crash dumps and then turning these dumps over to developers for analysis. In other situations, testers are responsible for both collecting and analyzing crash dump data.

Review Question

Which of the following are necessary to perform kernel debugging of a crashed test host machine in a Windows environment?

a. The Visual Studio integrated development environment program.

b. A .pdb file specific to the operating system on the test host, and also the windbg.exe GUI tool.

c. The universal windows.pdb file and also the kdbg.dll command line tool.

d. Just the cdb.exe command line tool.

6.6 The Windows System Registry

Each machine running a Windows operating system has a data store called the system registry. The registry holds many different kinds of information about applications installed on the machine. Because application installer programs often place information into the system registry and then the application reads that information during initialization, knowledge of the registry is particularly important for setup testing. The data in the system registry is stored internally in a binary format and so must be read and manipulated using the regedit.exe tool. System registry data is stored as pairs of data called keys and values. Keys are like variable names such as NoSearchBox. Values can be several different types. Two common registry value types are REG_SZ (a string such as "True") and REG_DWORD (an integer such as 1). One or more key-value pairs are contained in directory-like structures and these containers are hierarchically structured.

The system registry is organized into top-level logical groupings called hives. Examples of hives are HKEY_LOCAL_MACHINE (for machine-wide information) and HKEY_CURRENT_USER (for information specific to the current user logged onto the machine). For example, the Internet Explorer program displays a Search Box by default. To remove the Search Box display, a user can launch the regedit.exe program and navigate to the HKEY_ LOCAL_MACHINE \ Software \ Policies \ Microsoft \ Internet Explorer \ Infodelivery \ Restrictions data directory. That directory contains a Key named NoSearchBox which has a default value of type REG_DWORD set to 0. By changing that value to 1, the search box will not be displayed. Registry values can also be manipulated using text-based .reg data files in conjunction with the regedit.exe tool.

The system registry data is stored in multiple locations on a test host machine. The exact physical locations of data stores which make up the system registry vary depending upon which version of Windows is running on the test host machine. Most variants of the Unix operating system do not have an equivalent to the Windows registry application program global data store. In general, Unix variants store application data as ordinary text files in the etc/ directory and its subdirectories, and store user data in the /usr directory or the user's ~ home directory. On Windows systems, the use of such text files is a possible alternative to the system registry, and these files usually have an .ini (initialization) or .config (configuration) file extension.

Review Question

Suppose you are testing some software application on a Windows system. The application behaves differently depending upon the identity of the current logged on user. You suspect the problem may be in the system registry. Which of the following system registry values is most likely the cause of the behavior?

a. Hive=HKEY_LOCAL_MACHINE, Key=FullFunction, Value= REG_DWORD 0.

b. Hive=HKEY_LOCAL_MACHINE, Key=FullFunction, Value= RegistryTypeString 0.

c. Hive = HKEY_CURRENT_USER, Key=FullFunction, Value= REG_DWORD 0.

d. Hive=HKEY_CURRENT_USER, Key=FullFunction, Value= RegistryTypeString 0.

6.7 Stub Testing and Mock Testing

Stub testing is the process of creating a small, relatively simple placeholder method with very little if any functionality which can be called by the system under test. The term mock testing generally refers to a similar process where the placeholder is an OOP object and is created in part with the use of a code library. The concepts are best explained by example. Consider a system which makes airline flight reservations. A code snippet of a system which is designed using an OOP paradigm might look something like this:

```
Flight flt = new Flight("603");
string seat = "16e";
Reservation res = new Reservation();
res.Make(flt, seat);
// code to verify state
```

The first statement creates a Flight object, and the third and fourth statements make a seat reservation. Notice that in order to make a reservation, a Flight object must already exist. Now suppose you wish to test the method which makes a reservation but the Flight class has not yet been implemented. One solution is to create simple stub code along the lines of:

```
public class Flight {
 private string flightNumber;
 public Flight(string flightNumber) {
 this.flightNumber = "999";
 }
}
```

Here, the stub constructor merely assigns a dummy value to the flight number. Now a minimal Flight class exists and software test engineers can call and exercise the Reservation.Make() method to at least a minimal extent until the actual Flight class is implemented. In some testing scenarios stub code is created by testers with development skills, and in other scenarios testers make a request to the development team to create stub code for the purposes of testing. In general, the main problem with stub code is that because stub code has minimal logic and functionality, testing the methods in the SUT which rely on the stub code is often quite rudimentary. Of course stub code with complex functionality can be written but the level of development effort required to do so can be close to the level of effort necessary to implement the actual class being stubbed.

Mock object libraries are frameworks which help with the creation of stub code with some basic simulated functionality. Mock libraries exist for most common programming languages which support OOP design. Examples include NMock for the C# language and JMock for the Java language. Most mock libraries require that the system under development be designed using an interface-implementation paradigm. This means that each class is separated into an interface part which lists the methods in the class, and an implementation part which supplies the actual logic code. For example, testing the flight reservation system described above, where the Flight class has not yet been implemented might resemble something like:

```
IMock mockFlight = new
 DynamicMock(typeof(IFlight));
mockFlight.Expects( . . . );
string seat = "16e";
Reservation res = new Reservation();
res.makeFlight(mockFlight, seat);
mockFlight.Verify();
```

Notice that the creation of a mock object uses an interface. To summarize, in situations where classes in the SUT have not yet been implemented, testing with mock objects allows developers or test engineers to simplify the creation of placeholder code with a moderate amount of logic so that the system under development can be tested until the missing classes are completed.

Review Question

Which of the following statements is most often true about stub testing and mock testing?

a. In general, stub methods are more complex than mock objects. Stub methods are typically created with the help of a framework library, and mock objects are typically coded from scratch.

b. In general, stub methods are less complex than mock objects. Mock objects are typically created with the help of a framework library, and stub methods are typically coded from scratch.

c. In general, testing with stub methods requires that the system under test be designed and developed using the interface-implementation paradigm.

d. In general, testing with mock objects requires that the system under test be described with an XML schema file.

ANSWERS TO REVIEW QUESTIONS

Chapter 1 - Software Testing and Test Cases

1.1 Test Cases

c. { test case ID, constructor argument, three arguments for three calls to the Decrease() method, expected result value }.

This is the only set of information which contains data to set an initial state (the constructor argument), input values, and an expected result.

1.2 Equivalence Classes

a. { -10, 4, 16, 32 }.

This is the only set of values which contains one value from each of the four equivalence class: values less than 0, values between 0 and 10 inclusive, values between 11 and 19 inclusive, and values greater than 19.

1.3 Boundary Conditions

b. { minint, minint+1, -1, 0, 1, maxint-1, maxint }.

One of several natural ways to partition the set of integers is negative values, zero, and positive values. If the range of possible integer values on a system is limited to [minint, maxint], then there are three partitions: [minint, -1], [0], [1, maxint]. The values which are exactly at, just above, and just below the limits of the three partitions are those in answer set b.

1.4 Test Suites

b. BVTs are usually run after a new build of the system under development has been completed but before the build is released to test.

The tests in a BVT suite cannot be run until after a new build of the system under test has been created. BVT tests are run before the new build is released to test to ensure that the new build has some baseline level of functionality so that the build is in fact testable.

1.5 Code Coverage

b. Test suite B with 80% statement coverage.

Of function coverage, basic block coverage, statement coverage, decision, branch, and full path coverage, function coverage is the least detailed and provides the least amount of information, while full path coverage is the most detailed and provides the most information. Higher percentages of code coverage indicate more coverage.

1.6 Mutation Testing

a. Test suite A which initially yields 0 test case failures; 3,000 mutations which yield 500 additional test case failures.

Higher numbers of failures revealed by mutation testing indicates higher test suite effectiveness.

1.7 Static Code Analysis

e. None of the above.

Cyclomatic complexity is a static code analysis metric which measures the number of independent path of execution through a software module, based on the notion that modules with a large number of paths are likely to be more complex and therefore contain bugs, than modules with fewer paths.

Chapter 2 - Fundamental Mathematical Techniques

2.1 Measures of Central Tendency

c. For ratio data the geometric mean should be used.

For rate data, the harmonic mean should be used. For ordinary data the arithmetic mean, mode, or median should be used. Although there are exceptions to these guidelines, in most testing situations they hold true.

2.2 Measures of Variance

c. The population standard deviation.

Although often used, the range is relatively insensitive. Population measures are generally used more often than sample measures. Standard deviation is generally used more often than variance because the units of standard deviation are not squared unlike the variance.

2.3 Mathematical Permutations

b. Factorial(3) = 3! = 3 * 2 * 1 = 6.

Because there are three input values, there are 3! =6 ways to permute their order: {alpha, beta, gamma}, {alpha, gamma, beta}, {beta, alpha, gamma}, {beta, gamma, alpha}, {gamma, alpha, beta}, {gamma, beta, alpha}.

2.4 Mathematical Combinations

c. Choose(52,4) = (52 * 51 * 50 * 49) / (4 * 3 * 2 * 1).

This is one of several computational formulas for Chose(n,k).

2.5 Data Encryption

a. The plain text is encoded using a public key, and the resulting cipher text is decoded using an associated private key.

RSA is a public key encryption algorithm.

2.6 Crypto-Hashing

c. The size of the output is always 20 bytes regardless of the size of the input.

Crypto-hash algorithms such MD5 and SHA-1 have a fixed output size. MD5 is an older algorithm and considered somewhat less secure than the newer SHA-1 algorithm.

2.7 Pair-Wise Testing

b. 26 test cases.

There is no quick formula which computes the number of pairs which must be captured for a given input set. For the stated problem, the 26 pairs are:

(a,e), (a,f), (a,g), (a,h), (a,i),

(b,e), (b,f), (b,g), (b,h), (b,i),

(c,e), (c,f), (c,g), (c,h), (c,i),

(d,e), (d,f), (d,g), (d,h), (d,i),

(e,g), (e,h), (e,i),

(f,g), (f,h), (f,i).

Chapter 3 - Project Management Concepts

3.1 The Software Development Life Cycle

d. A variation of the agile software development methodology paradigm.

Although agile software development methodologies can use formal documentation and traditional project management techniques, in most cases they do not.

3.2 Project Management Constraints

c. Quality is often considered part of the scope constraint.

The triple constraints are time, cost, and scope. Quality is generally either considered part of scope, or a separate fourth constraint.

3.3 Beta Distribution Estimation

d. Determine optimistic, pessimistic, and most likely case estimates, then use the Beta distribution to compute an overall estimate, and report all four values.

This option provides the most information for an estimate.

3.4 Test Effort Documentation

d. Test Log.

In the IEEE 829 standard, the Test Log is intended to hold details of which tests cases were run, when they were run, and a pass / fail result.

3.5 Source and Version Control Tools

d. All of the above.

An advantage of using sophisticated source/version control tools such as CVS is that they typically store all previous versions of the SUD, allow separate paths of development, and permit merging of separate paths.

3.6 Bug Reports

c. A bug with severity = 1 and priority = 4.

In many situation the severity and priority fields for a bug have the same values. Sometimes a low severity bug may have a high priority if the bug is blocking development or testing progress. It is least common to have a high severity bug with a low priority because high severity bugs are often crashing or hanging bugs and must be fixed quickly.

3.7 Reproduction Steps

b. The description field is generally longer than the title field.

The description field can be thought of as an expanded title. Spelling errors in the title or description can easily lead to duplicate bug entries. Spelling errors in the comment field, while not good, are less likely to lead to a duplicate entry.

Chapter 4 - Core Principles

4.1 Black Box and White Box Testing

c. In general, use of the term white box or black box may be somewhat useful on a software testing job description to help a human resources department categorize the extent to which the job position requires project management skills.

Both black box and white box testing approaches are usually required for a thorough test effort.

4.2 Manual and Automated Testing

d. All of the above.

According to the SAPES principle, compared to manual testing, automated testing has greater speed, better accuracy, superior precision, is more efficient, and facilitates skill-building.

4.3 Stress and Load Testing

c. Testing a software system using normal functionality test cases, while the system is operating under a condition of reduced CPU availability due to a processor-intensive dummy application running on the test host machine.

Stress testing usually exercises the system under test when operating under conditions of low CPU availability, low RAM, or limited hard drive space.

4.4 Configuration Testing

d. In most cases the number of different configurations is far too large to thoroughly test; therefore the test plan should prioritize which configurations will be tested, and which configurations will not be tested.

Application software such as the types described in the question can be run in a huge number of different hardware and software configurations.

4.5 Localization Testing

d. Internationalization is the process of designing a software system so that it can be easily translated into multiple languages; localization is the actual process of translating a software system into a particular language and culture (such as Canada French or Belgium French).

Although the terms internationalization and localization are sometimes used interchangeably in informal communication, they are better defined as above.

4.6 Record-Playback Testing

b. In general, record-playback UI testing provides little value to a testing effort except for relatively simple regression testing scenarios.

This statement is an opinion based on survey data. However there are experienced software test engineers who have alternative opinions which hold record-playback testing in higher regard.

4.7 Random Input Testing

c. In most situations with random input testing, it is not possible to have an explicit expected result, so the implicit expected result is a system crash, hang, or exception of some sort.

In most situations the pseudorandom number generator is initialized with some arbitrary but specific seed value so that the test run and results are reproducible.

Chapter 5 - Essential Knowledge

5.1 Character Encoding

Which of the following is the correct UTF-8 Unicode encoding for character 'z' (lower case letter z which has ASCII value 122d = 7Ah = 01111010b)?

a. 0111 1010

For characters with codes in the range 0d - 255d, UTF-8 encoding uses 8 bits and the same bit encoding as ASCII.

5.2 XML and Testing

Which of the following technologies is commonly used to transform XML from one format to another?

c. XSLT (Extensible Stylesheet Language Transformations).

XSD and DTD files are normally used for XML validation. XQuery is generally used to extract data from an XML file.

5.3 HTTP Request-Response Testing

Which of the following represents a valid test case input when typed into the address bar of a Web browser?

a. http://localhost/buildPage.asp::city=Bay City::state=RI

b. http://localhost/buildPage.asp/city/Bay,City/state/RI

c. http://localhost/buildPage.asp?city=Bay+City&state=RI

d. http://localhost/buildPage.asp\\city,Bay%20City\\state,RI

Answer = c.

Query strings consist of a URL followed by a '?' delimiting character and then a list of name-value pairs in the form of name=value, delimited by the '&' character.

5.4 HTTP State Testing

a. Examine the Cookies on the two client machines' hard drives to see if there are any differences.

Application State objects on the Web server would likely affect all users of the Web application.

5.5 Testing Database-Centric Applications

a. In order to test the application you will likely need to create a testbed database which is different from the development database and different from the production database.

Using the production database for testing purposes could destroy or corrupt important data. Development databases often do not contain data which is designed to allow thorough testing.

5.6 Copying Files

a. C:\Gamma> net use x: \\Beta\Public

C:\Gamma> xcopy C:\Data\Tests*.txt x:

C:\Gamma> net use /delete x:

This is the only answer with correct syntax and legal commands.

5.7 Network Troubleshooting

a. Perform a Windows Repair of the local host machine using the original operating system installation disk.

b. Attempt to access a different remote machine using the local host machine.

c. Replace the NIC (network interface card) on the local host machine.

d. Reboot the local host machine.

Answer = b.

In general, the first troubleshooting steps should be those which are relatively quick and easy, and those which reveal the most common causes of the problem.

Chapter 6 - Units, Modules, and Components

6.1 Dynamic Link Libraries

d. A ProgId for the DLL for use by scripting languages.

The entries in the Windows system registry for a dual-interface COM component include an ID in the form of a GUID, physical location of the component, and a ProgID identifier for use by scripting languages.

6.2 The Global Assembly Cache

c. gacutil.exe

The sn.exe tool is used to create a strong name. The cmd.exe program in conjunction with the dir command can be used to view the contents of the GAC in raw form, but using the gacitil.exe program with a /l argument is usually a better option.

6.3 Module Testing

d. All of the above.

One of the characteristics of COM technology is that it can be used to create a component which can be called by different languages, including scripting languages, when the component is implemented using a dual-interface approach.

6.4 Unit Testing

c. Unit testing is primarily a developer activity and is typically used to test methods of the system under test during system development.

Unit testing can be used by testers and managers, but is most often used by developers as part of the so-called test driven development methodology.

6.5 Kernel Debugging

b. A .pdb file specific to the operating system on the test host, and also the windbg.exe GUI tool.

Kernel debugging requires a .pdb file which is specific to the operating machine on the system which is being debugged. The windbg.exe tool is essentially a GUI wrapper around command line programs including the kdb.exe kernel debugger program. Neither Visual Studio nor the cdb.exe program can directly perform kernel debugging.

6.6 The Windows System Registry

c. Hive = HKEY_CURRENT_USER, Key = FullFunction, Value = REG_DWORD 0.

In general, registry settings in the HKEY_LOCAL_MACHINE hive apply to the entire host machine and all users. Registry settings in the HKEY_CURRENT_USER hive are intended to apply only to the currently logged-on user. Common registry value types are REG_DWORD and REG_SZ. There is no RegistryTypeString value type.

6.7 Stub Testing and Mock Testing

b. In general, stub methods are less complex than mock objects. Mock objects are typically created with the help of a framework library, and stub methods are typically coded from scratch.

Although mock objects can be coded from scratch, they are usually implemented with the help of a mock object framework library such as NMock or JMock.

INDEX

1684915R00063

Made in the USA
San Bernardino, CA
16 January 2013